Kingdom Builders
PLAYBOOK

*Ultimate Guide for Leadership, Investing,
Stewardship, and Taxes*

Ryan Bourque, CPA, MBT, CKA

WESTBOW
P R E S S®
A DIVISION OF THOMAS NELSON
& ZONDERVAN

WestBow Press books may be ordered through booksellers or by contacting:

WestBow Press
A Division of Thomas Nelson & Zondervan
1663 Liberty Drive
Bloomington, IN 47403
www.westbowpress.com
844-714-3454

ISBN: 979-8-3850-0816-2 (sc)
ISBN: 979-8-3850-0860-5 (hc)
ISBN: 979-8-3850-0861-2 (e)

Library of Congress Control Number: 2023918283

Print information available on the last page.

WestBow Press rev. date: 09/29/2023

Acknowledgments

Foremost, I would like to express my deepest gratitude to my family and friends for their unwavering support and encouragement throughout the writing of this book. Special thanks to John Apuzzo, CPA; Chuck McLucas, CPA; David Keligian, JD/CPA; and Hank Adler, CPA. My career spent working with you as friends and associates helped me work with clients to effectively advise on their finances, businesses, and estates while encompassing their faith in their decision-making.

My editor played a crucial role in helping me shape and refine this manuscript. For that, I am deeply appreciative.

Thank you to the pastors and authors who sparked the ideas for this book through their insights, advice, and feedback.

Above all, I want to express my heartfelt thanks to the readers who will give this book their time and attention. I hope this work will benefit you and inspire you to greater heights.

I also want to acknowledge and thank all the individuals who have inspired and encouraged me throughout this journey we call life. Your unwavering support and guidance have been the backbone of my success.

I want to thank Pastor Rick Warren, Pastor Dave Arnold, and Pastor Chris Goulard from Saddleback Church. I have been a member of Saddleback Church for over twenty years and have had the utmost privilege of mentorship from just about the greatest minds in Christian stewardship and leadership. They helped me realize my potential and what it means to be a kingdom builder.

A final note of appreciation goes to the publishing team, who worked tirelessly behind the scenes to bring this book to life. Thank you all for your efforts, from the editorial to the design, production, and marketing team.

Contents

Foreword

We are called each by our unique gifts and abilities to be a part of the body of Christ, which is the Christian church. I don't speak of a building or other dogma, but the movement of men and women after God's heart that are touched in a unique God-given way. Everything is from God, and it is up to you to explore what your gifts are and how they can further God's kingdom here on earth.

> We have gifts that differ according to the grace given to us: prophecy, in proportion to faith; ministry, in ministering; the teacher, in teaching; the exhorter, in exhortation; the giver, in generosity; the leader, in diligence; the compassionate, in cheerfulness (Romans 12:6–8, NRSV).

Being a kingdom builder is not just a term; it speaks to the heart of who we are as Christian leaders and stewards. It is a calling of the highest order for those given the gifts of leadership and generosity. A group of Christ followers that seek to always turn their successes into eternal significance with a kingdom impact here on earth and in heaven.

A kingdom builder is someone who has been transformed by the Gospel of Christ and desires to build God's kingdom on earth and to be an integral part of His unfolding plan. This means fulfilling the Great Commission and using our gifts of leadership and generosity to bring hope and love to the world by living more and more like Jesus Christ by His grace.

Being a kingdom builder boils down to stewardship—stewardship of all that is entrusted to us. Whether it is through leadership in business or through financial giving, the unavoidable tool is money. Money is not just a financial resource but a spiritual resource that God has entrusted us with. Money was a pivotal topic in the Bible. Jesus spoke more about money and possessions than He did about heaven or hell. How we handle our finances, whether in our personal lives, business ownership, or philanthropic endeavors, has an eternal impact beyond the short sixty-five to one hundred years we spend here on earth.

To build God's kingdom financially, we must understand and apply biblical money principles and develop a mindset of keeping an eternal perspective and always putting true ownership at the forefront of our decisions. When it comes to ownership, remember that it all comes from God and belongs to God.

This playbook breaks down the fundamentals of being a kingdom builder into the areas of leadership, stewardship, and taxes.

As Christians, let us strive to be kingdom builders in every aspect of our lives. Let us hold our time, talent, and treasure with open hands and use them to advance God's kingdom. May the principles, strategies, and examples outlined in this guide inspire and equip you to be a faithful steward of God's blessings and make a kingdom impact in the world around you.

Blessings,
Ryan Bourque, CPA, MB.T, CKA

1

Why Am I Here on Earth?

I was an eighteen-year-old attending Chapman University when a car accident permanently damaged my spine. I was missing school to go to physical therapy and meet with doctors—trying to restore my health and life. Without realizing or knowing what it was, I fell into a deep depression.

A high school classmate who attended college with me told me about Saddleback Church and this new book, *The Purpose Driven Life,* written by their senior pastor, Rick Warren. Seeking meaning in my life, I decided to check out this church. I was working weekends and asked my boss if I could leave early to attend their last Sunday service.

It was God's perfect timing.

Being used to going to a Mormon Church, then a Catholic Church, and attending chapel at my Christian school, this megachurch seemed like Disneyland. Shuttles were transporting people from the parking lot to the worship center. Various tents and venues cater to different music styles and worship experiences. I'll never forget the warm welcome received from the greeters as you made the long trek from the parking lot up the stairs by the fountains into the worship center.

Pastor Rick Warren was teaching a sermon, and it felt like he spoke directly to me. It's a common occurrence for most people who hear his sermons for the first time. His practical applications of biblical principles laid out a model of how I would approach my personal and spiritual life, career, and ministry.

The Age-Old Question

I don't have strong enough faith to believe that everything in this universe happens accidentally. I don't believe that something comes from nothing. And I certainly don't have the ability to be an atheist and say that I am a hundred percent sure that there is no God and no rhyme or reason to this earth or all of creation.

Certain things in this world comfort me and reinforce my belief in the existence of God. Music is one of my strongest arguments. We can't find shelter, eat, or evolve based on our love for music. Music helps tell a story of our experience as humans on this planet. Just because we don't understand everything in this universe doesn't mean there isn't a Creator.

I also challenge the notion that just because I can't see something means it doesn't exist. In a rare exception, some people have seen the face of God, but most of us haven't seen Him nor heard Him audibly. Some of the most prominent pastors in America have clearly made it known that they have never heard God audibly. However, they experience the power and prompting of the Holy Spirit, and those impressions are tested through proper means.

Furthermore, modern technology astounds me. It is incredible to me that images, songs, and voices pass through the air and through us. I am still blown away that I can send a photo from my phone in real-time halfway across the planet. Just because I don't understand the technology and can't physically see it doesn't mean it isn't real. Though we are created in God's image, we are not God, nor will we ever be. Only God understands His plan, and how everything is woven together; we do not. We are like an ant trying to understand the internet.

KINGDOM BUILDERS PLAYBOOK

What Is the Meaning of Life?

I subscribe to the view of my pastor of twenty years on the meaning of life as outlined in his best-selling book, *The Purpose Driven Life*. It is a spiritual self-help book that inspires readers to discover their unique purpose in life. The book is based on biblical principles and emphasizes the importance of trusting God's plan, developing a relationship with Jesus, and serving others. Life's purpose is not just to live for your benefit but to contribute to the betterment of the world.

This comprehensive guide to living with intention and purpose inspired me to focus on my relationship with God, discover His unique plan for my life, live according to my values and beliefs, and serve others.

I've read and revisited *The Purpose Driven Life* many times—it has been a practical guide in my life. I don't think I'll ever perfectly balance life's five purposes, worship, unselfish fellowship, spiritual maturity, ministry, and mission. But I'm not sure anybody does—at least not in this life.

Discovering Your Kingdom Builder Strengths

If I know I am created for God's pleasure and to serve and love others, how do I determine what I am supposed to do with my life or what I would even be good at doing?

A great way to learn what drives you is by taking a Myers-Briggs personality test. Exploring the four dimensions, which encompass the focal point of attention, information processing, decision-making, and dealing with the world, provided me with valuable insights about myself. Although ENTJ (my personality type)—the Commander—and INTJ (Elon Musk) are natural kingdom builders, all personality types have the traits to become kingdom builders.

Personality tests can help you understand yourself better—strengths and weaknesses—and how to interact with others. However, people are multidimensional, and personality types serve as broad descriptions rather than strict definitions; you are uniquely made by God.

Another helpful resource was discovering my S.H.A.P.E.—the acronym for Spiritual Gifts, Heart, Abilities, Personality, and Experiences. Taught in Class 301 at Saddleback Church and outlined in Erik Rees's book *S.H.A.P.E.,* this concept encourages you to take a personal inventory of your S.H.A.P.E. It took me years before I attended Class 301 for reasons I don't know why I procrastinated. It helped me determine my gifts and how to apply them to life's five purposes in fulfillment of the Great Commission and Great Commandment.

If you are reading this book, you are likely interested in discovering your ministry. There are so many ministry opportunities to get involved in that serve to further God's kingdom here on earth and to live out the Great Commission and the Great Commandment.

I have had the blessing of being a blessing to others through opportunities that I have had through the church and work for charity. Though I have done it, painting and repairing homes and church facilities weren't what I felt was my potential. I believe there is room in the church and God's kingdom for everyone to contribute in their own unique way.

Leading up to writing this book and launching the Kingdom Builders Ministries, Inc. Non-profit was a long path of self-discovery, life experience, and quite the journey of learning about biblical leadership, stewardship, and generosity and gaining so much even more than the participants I've been facilitating and teaching about the subject. You learn more by hosting and training than you ever imagined possible.

While carrying eighteen units as a college junior, I worked full-time for a CPA firm. I found a lot of purpose in what I did in helping people and was able to apply what I was learning in school to my newfound career choice.

I graduated from Chapman University with a bachelor's degree in accounting and married my college sweetheart. Then I went on to study to obtain my CPA license in California. In addition to helping run a thriving tax practice, I began teaching for Becker Professional Education to help prepare students to succeed in their careers and pass their CPA exams. During this time, I received my master's degree in tax from the University of Southern California (USC).

While plugging along in my career, the University of California, Irvine program director approached me to help create an online applied accounting program. I developed the entire curriculum for the program with the design that graduates would go on to successfully pass the CPA exam. I taught for that program for several years and still serve as a subject matter expert and an advisory board member at the time of this publishing.

As I was already building my professional resume, I was also developing my ministry skills at Saddleback Church, where I'd attended since I was eighteen. After a major medical setback and debilitating medical diagnosis, I decided to dedicate more time to ministry. I joined the Financial Freedom (Stewardship) Ministry to become involved beyond only attending church on Sundays and being a small group host.

The Financial Freedom Ministries provides counseling, workshops, seminars, and Bible studies on stewardship and biblical money management. I was involved in that ministry for about ten years, moving up in responsibilities to facilitate ministry offerings of live classes. I became part of the leadership group of this ministry and thoroughly enjoyed my volunteer work.

My good friend Pastor Chris Goulard transitioned from running the Financial Freedom Ministry to the newly created Saddleback Church Kingdom Builders Ministry, co-facilitated by Pastor Dave Arnold. I was excited about the prospect of this ministry as I had spent years talking with Pastor Goulard about starting a group or ministry of high-capacity church members that could have fellowship and grow with each other for those gifted with leadership and generosity.

In launching this ministry, one aspect of reaching the members of Saddleback's Kingdom Builders Ministry was my hosting and facilitating Journey of Generosity retreats created by a nonprofit called Generous Giving. Through these retreats, high-capacity kingdom builders could explore their life stories of money, possessions, and stewardship, make friends, and put their lives into perspective that God owns it all and that we are the stewards of the resources entrusted to us.

Saddleback's Kingdom Builders Ministry was in its infancy, and we were all brainstorming. I shared many unsolicited ideas about ministry and how to engage the members and the kingdom builders group. Ultimately pastors met with kingdom builders individually to minister to them and guide them in their walk with the Lord and in their leadership and generosity. We also had quarterly get-togethers with speakers who engaged the group and got us thinking about our purpose and how to use our unique talents and gifts to impact the world.

I spent some time, in addition to Saddleback, attending a smaller church. I was awoken to the fact that most churches do not have stewardship ministries and surely do not have Kingdom Builders' Ministries. I wrote this book to tell my story and help launch a ministry with resources to help others start a Kingdom Builders' Ministry in their local church or community.

What Is a Balanced Kingdom Builder?

Being a balanced kingdom builder means consistently living a life guided by biblical principles and God's truth. It requires a holistic and integrated approach to life, where all areas of your life are aligned with God's Word.

A balanced kingdom builder strives for balance in your spiritual, personal, family, and professional life, seeking to honor God in all areas. This pursuit involves seeking God daily through prayer, Bible reading, fostering fellowship with other believers, and attending church regularly.

It also means caring for your physical and emotional health, practicing self-care, and cultivating healthy relationships with others. This may involve seeking professional assistance when needed, getting wise counsel from trusted Christian friends and mentors, and prioritizing rest, recreation, and healthy habits.

Regarding family life, a balanced kingdom builder seeks to love and serve your spouse sacrificially, cherishing them as a precious gift from God. A kingdom builder strives to be present and engaged in children's lives, modeling God's love, grace, and discipline. A kingdom builder also serves as a spiritual leader, guiding their family in their relationships with God and their Christian walk.

Finally, being a balanced kingdom builder involves being a responsible and productive member of society, diligently working to provide for your family, and actively serving in the community as Christ's ambassador. A balanced kingdom builder is a person of integrity, values, and purpose who seeks to make a positive difference in the world and impact those around him for the kingdom of God.

This book is primarily intended for Christians with the gift of generosity and leadership. If this resonates with you and is who you aspire to be, I hope this playbook sparks your imagination to envision what is possible in your life.

Always remember, you are not an accident. You have been given a unique set of God-given talents and abilities. God knew in the creation of the cosmos that you would be reading this book right now and exploring what it is that makes you one of a kind and how you can take who you are and where you have been to have a lasting impact on building God's kingdom here on earth.

SECTION 1

LEADERSHIP

2

Biblical Principles in Decision-Making

As a leader, steering discussions and making decisions are core responsibilities of your role. However, it is easy to rely solely on your abilities and understanding, leading to hasty decisions without considering the biblical context or adhering to proper procedures.

People often face difficult choices in life, and determining the best course of action can be challenging. When making decisions, Christians have the unique advantage of drawing upon biblical principles that offer invaluable guidance and direction.

Integrating biblical principles into the decision-making process gives you, as a kingdom builder, an added dimension of clarity and purpose. You are blessed with this treasure trove of biblical wisdom, a gift you can access to uphold the values of your faith and align your decisions with God's desires.

Seeking God's Will

The pivotal starting point of the decision-making process for believers is seeking God's will.

> Therefore do not be foolish, but understand what the Lord's will is (Ephesians 5:17, NIV).

Recognizing that God is the source of all wisdom, and by seeking Him, you have clarity and direction in your decision-making process.

> Those who trust in themselves are fools, but those who walk in wisdom are kept safe (Proverbs 28:26, NIV).

> The simple believe anything, but the prudent give thought to their steps (Proverbs 14:15, NIV).

The Holy Spirit of Truth guides you to live wisely, and the Bible encourages you to seek God's wisdom to live according to His will.

> If anyone, then, knows the good they ought to do and doesn't do it, it is sin for them (James 4:17, NIV).

God's Word as a Guide

The Bible serves as the primary source of guidance for believers. It provides a framework of principles and values when making decisions. Reading the Bible regularly and applying the teachings to everyday situations offers clarity and direction. Always consider what the Bible has to say about the topic.

> But it was to us that God revealed these things by his Spirit. For his Spirit searches out everything and shows us God's deep secrets. No one can know a person's thoughts except that person's own spirit, and no one can know God's thoughts except God's own Spirit. And we have received God's Spirit (not the world's spirit), so we can know the wonderful things God has freely given us. When we tell you these things, we do not use words that come from human wisdom. Instead, we speak words given to us by the Spirit, using the Spirit's words to explain spiritual truths (1 Corinthians 2:10–13, NLT).

The Role of Prayer

Prayer plays a significant role in decision-making as it helps you to stay connected to God and receive divine guidance. Prayer can also offer clarity and peace, allowing you to confidently make decisions. If you ask, seek, and knock on God's door for direction, He will answer you.

> Ask, and it will be given to you; seek, and you will find; knock, and it will be opened to you. For everyone who asks receives, and he who seeks finds, and to him who knocks it will be opened (Matthew 7:7–8, NKJV).

The Lord's Prayer

The Lord's Prayer is your model for prayer. This prayer serves as a template for understanding the different aspects of prayer, including praise, adoration, seeking God's will, and seeking forgiveness.

> In this manner, therefore, pray: Our Father in heaven, hallowed be Your name. Your kingdom come. Your will be done on earth as it is in heaven. Give us this day our daily bread. And forgive us our debts, as we forgive our debtors. And do not lead us into temptation, but deliver us from the evil one. For Yours is the kingdom and the power and the glory forever. Amen (Matthew 6:9–13, NKJV).

Prayer Is a Conversation

Approach prayer as a conversation with God. Listening to God's voice, expressing gratitude, and sharing your deepest concerns and desires with Him is important.

> You can be sure of this: The Lord set apart the godly for himself. The Lord will answer when I call to him (Psalm 4:3, NLT).

Praying with Faith

Faith in God's ability to answer prayers is a crucial aspect of prayer. Faith should be rooted in understanding God's nature and His promises found in the Bible.

> Let us draw near with a true heart in full assurance of faith, having our hearts sprinkled from an evil conscience and our bodies washed with pure water (Hebrews 10:22, NKJV).

Praying for God's Will

Align your desires with God's will while praying. The Bible encourages you to surrender your desires and submit to God's plans; trusting His way is ultimately best.

> And we are confident that he hears us whenever we ask for anything that pleases him. And since we know he hears us when we make our requests, we also know that he will give us what we ask for (1 John 5:14–15, NLT).

Persistence in Prayer

Continue to pray even when your prayers seem unanswered. Jesus tells a parable about the need to persist in prayer.

> One day Jesus told his disciples a story to show that they should always pray and never give up. "There was a judge in a certain city," He said, "who neither feared God nor cared about people. A widow of that city came to him repeatedly, saying, 'Give me justice in this dispute with my enemy.' The judge ignored her for a while, but finally he said to himself, 'I don't fear God or care about people, but this woman is driving me crazy. I'm going to see that

she gets justice, because she is wearing me out with her constant requests!'"

Then the Lord said, "Learn a lesson from this unjust judge. Even he rendered a just decision in the end. So don't you think God will surely give justice to his chosen people who cry out to him day and night? Will he keep putting them off? I tell you, he will grant justice to them quickly! But when the Son of Man returns, how many will he find on the earth who have faith?" (Luke 18:1–8, NLT).

Praying for Others

Pastor Warren taught me the power of intercessory prayer, where you pray on behalf of others. Praying for others aligns with God's heart of love and is a meaningful way to express care and support for others.

Confess to one another therefore your faults (your slips, your false steps, your offenses, your sins) and pray [also] for one another, that you may be healed and restored [to a spiritual tone of mind and heart]. The earnest (heartfelt, continued) prayer of a righteous man makes tremendous power available [dynamic in its working] (James 5:16, AMPC).

Seeking Wise Counsel

Plans fail for lack of counsel, but with many advisers, they succeed (Proverbs 15:22, NIV).

Seeking input from people with more experience or expertise can provide valuable insight and guidance when making decisions. But first, ask the Holy Spirit's guidance.

However, when He, the Spirit of truth, has come, He will guide you into all truth; for He will not speak on His own

authority, but whatever He hears He will speak; and He
will tell you things to come (John 16:13, NKJV).

I have had the utmost luxury of being able to seek counsel from several
pastors who are friends and clients and through close Christian friends.
I strongly suggest you evaluate the company you keep and come to the
understanding that seeing things from multiple Christian viewpoints and
seeing the Holy Spirit speak to you through other believers is an absolute
necessity.

For where two or three have gathered together in My
name, I am there in their midst (Matthew 18:20, NASB).

Evaluating the Consequences

Evaluating the potential consequences of decisions is essential. It helps you
consider the impact of your decision on yourself and others and whether
it aligns with biblical values and principles. By listening to the warnings
and promptings of your conscience, you can avoid making poor decisions.

In view of this, I also do my best and strive always to
have a clear conscience before God and before men (Acts
24:16, AMP).

Therefore, since we know the fear of the Lord [and
understand the importance of obedience and worship],
we persuade people [to be reconciled to Him]. But we are
plainly known to God [He knows everything about us]; and
I hope that we are plainly known also in your consciences
[your God-given discernment] (2 Corinthians 5:11, AMP).

I have always had the gift of foresight; seeing what lies ahead is easy. It
is even easier for me to see the potential pitfalls and dangers over the
benefits of most decisions. I suggest you seek the counsel of Christian-
based professionals, like consultants, CPAs, lawyers, or financial advisors.
I encourage you to check out the group Kingdom Advisors (Kingdom
Advisors.com) to help build your team of wise counsel.

God's Guidance

When you seek God's guidance, He promises to guide you and provide practical steps. God is always with you. He promises His presence, and His Holy Spirit dwells in you, guiding and directing your path.

> And the Lord will guide you continually and satisfy your desire in scorched places and make your bones strong; and you shall be like a watered garden, like a spring of water, whose waters do not fail (Isaiah 58:11, ESV).

God has the perfect plan and purpose for your life.

> "For I know the plans that I have for you," declares the Lord, "plans for prosperity and not for disaster, to give you a future and a hope," (Jeremiah 29:11, NASB).

You are not alone when making decisions; you can always rely on God's wisdom and guidance. God's wisdom surpasses all human understanding, and He gives you insight when you seek it. Ask for God's guidance and trust His wisdom when your path is uncertain.

Trusting God's Sovereignty

Trust in God's sovereignty in all decision-making processes is essential. Christians recognize that God works all things together for the good of those who love Him. Trusting in God's sovereignty offers peace, comfort, and confidence, even when decisions may result in less-than-optimal outcomes.

Applying biblical principles in decision-making is not a formula but a lifestyle. A kingdom builder recognizes that good decision-making requires dependence on God's wisdom and guidance. By consulting God's Word, seeking wise counsel, evaluating potential consequences, and wholly trusting God's sovereignty, you align your decisions with God's will and contribute to the advancement of His kingdom.

3

Kingdom Builder Leadership

The true essence of a kingdom builder's leadership is selfless dedication to God's glory building His Kingdom on earth. It is deeply rooted in biblical principles and teachings that guide a kingdom builder's leadership approach and characteristics.

Character Traits of Christian Leadership

Certain character traits, principles, and values define effective Christian leaders. Jesus Christ's life and teachings show how to lead with a kingdom mindset, empowering others to join in the divine mission of building God's kingdom on earth.

Visionary Leadership

Visionary leadership is a vital element of a kingdom builder leader. As an innovative leader, you develop a compelling vision for the future, inspiring and motivating your team to embrace the shared vision. Strategic planning, setting goals, outlining action steps, assessing progress, and allocating resources help realize this vision.

You can adapt plans and strategies as needed, staying flexible in response to changing circumstances and new information. With persistence and resilience, a kingdom builder leader faces challenges, encourages creative thinking, and continues moving forward despite setbacks and obstacles.

Kingdom Builder's Heart

The heart of a kingdom builder is a surrendered servanthood; it's embracing the selfless attitude of a servant and following Jesus's example of humility and sacrificial love. A kingdom builder aligns leadership decisions and actions with God's purposes by having a kingdom vision. You must cultivate a vibrant and intimate relationship with the Lord to seek God's guidance and empowering presence in all leadership endeavors.

In addition, a kingdom business leader serves others by meeting customer needs, empowering employees, and contributing to the community. You achieve this by creating value for others, having a customer-centric approach, and building solid stakeholder relationships.

Kingdom Impact

To be a Christian leader in your community means that you seek to make a positive difference in the lives of those around you through the power of Christ's love. You reflect God's love and bring about positive change by engaging with and serving the local community's needs.

As a Christian, you are called to be salt and light in the world, representing Christ's character in all your interactions with others.

> You are the salt of the earth. But if the salt loses its saltiness, how can it be made salty again? It is no longer good for anything, except to be thrown out and trampled underfoot. You are the light of the world. A town built on a hill cannot be hidden. Neither do people light a lamp and put it under a bowl. Instead they put it on its stand, and it gives light to everyone in the house. In the same way,

let your light shine before others, that they may see your
good deeds and glorify your Father in heaven (Matthew
5:13–16, NIV).

Integrity and Compassion

Being a Christian leader in your community requires living a life of integrity
and compassion, striving to fulfill the Great Commission and the Great
Commandment by loving God and loving your neighbor as yourself. This
means being a faithful witness to your faith, sharing the gospel with those who
do not know Christ, and demonstrating His love through service and kindness.

The foundation of leadership is a Christ-like character of prioritizing
integrity, authenticity, and moral excellence. A compassionate leader
demonstrates empathy, care, and genuine concern for the needs and
aspirations of others.

Peacemaker

Seek to be a peacemaker in your community, building bridges and creating
partnerships that promote unity and understanding across diverse groups.
Strive to advocate for justice, stand up for the oppressed and marginalized,
and champion the cause of righteousness and mercy.

So then, let us pursue [with enthusiasm] the things which
make for peace and the building up of one another [things
which lead to spiritual growth] (Romans 14:19, AMP).

Deceit fills hearts that are plotting evil; joy fills hearts that
are planning peace! (Proverbs 12:20, NLT).

Empowering Kingdom Builders

Kingdom builder leaders equip and empower individuals in their sphere of
influence by identifying and developing their gifts, talents, and potential.

Mentoring and discipleship are vital in empowering kingdom builders. By investing in the growth and development of emerging leaders, you can guide and support them on their kingdom-building journey.

This fosters an environment that encourages collaboration, teamwork, and a shared commitment to advancing God's kingdom. By multiplying kingdom builders, you are replicating the kingdom-building vision and empowering others to become leaders and influencers in their spheres of influence.

Wisdom and Discernment

Seeking Godly wisdom is key for any Christian leader. Through prayer, seek His wisdom and counsel, and study His Word for decision-making guidance.

> But the wisdom from above is first of all pure (undefiled); then it is peace-loving, courteous (considerate, gentle). [It is willing to] yield to reason, full of compassion and good fruits; it is wholehearted and straightforward, impartial and unfeigned (free from doubts, wavering, and insincerity) (James 3:17, AMPC).

> If any of you lacks wisdom [to guide him through a decision or circumstance], he is to ask of [our benevolent] God, who gives to everyone generously and without rebuke or blame, and it will be given to him (James 1:5, AMP).

When you are sensitive to the leading of the Holy Spirit, you can discern the direction and timing of God's plans for your kingdom-building initiatives. You become bold and courageous kingdom builders, stepping out in faith and embracing the risk when God leads, trusting in His provision and guidance.

Delegation and Teambuilding

Learning to delegate and building teams are two vital kingdom builder leadership characteristics. Doing everything yourself is not a productive way to spend your time, and you may feel overwhelmed, isolated, and unfulfilled. In addition, you are not allowing others to grow and express their skills and expertise.

It took me a long time to realize the importance of building teams and delegation. Once I grasped the essence, it freed up my time. It empowered others to contribute their expertise and input to the business. By promoting unity, trust, and clarity, individuals can work together harmoniously, increasing productivity and success.

Respect, same values, and open communication help create unity in a team. Agreement occurs when team members put personal interests aside to work together toward a common goal.

A successful team's foundation is trust. Building trust among team members requires transparency, honesty, and dependability. I learned to create a positive work environment by trusting and empowering my team members.

Effective communication and clearly defining goals and objectives clarify each team member's role and responsibility. Regularly assessing the team's progress and making necessary adjustments ensures everyone is on the same page.

Ultimately, being a Christian leader in your community means living out your faith in every aspect of your life, pursuing excellence, and striving to reach your God-given potential. Seek to be an ambassador for Christ, representing Him well and making Him known to all who cross your path.

Servant Leadership

Servant leadership is a leadership style based on serving others selflessly and sacrificially. True servant leadership is modeled after the example of Jesus Christ, who served others with humility, love, and compassion.

Jesus emphasized servant leadership as the ideal model for His followers. In Matthew 20:25–28, Jesus taught that the greatest among them should be the servant of all. This teaching promotes a leadership style that prioritizes serving and meeting the needs of others rather than seeking power or authority.

> But Jesus called them to Himself and said, "You know that the rulers of the Gentiles lord it over them, and those who are great exercise authority over them. Yet it shall not be so among you; but whoever desires to become great among you, let him be your servant. And whoever desires to be first among you, let him be your slave—just as the Son of Man did not come to be served, but to serve, and to give His life a ransom for many" (Matthew 20:25–28, NKJV).

Putting Others First

As a servant leader, you prioritize the needs and interests of others above your own and work to meet the physical, emotional, and spiritual needs of those around you. You demonstrate genuine care and concern for the well-being and growth of those you lead. In addition, you seek opportunities to serve others, partnering with organizations that seek to impact society positively.

Humility

A servant leader displays humility, recognizing that leadership is not about seeking personal power or recognition. You must be willing to set aside your own ego and serve with a spirit of humility. The New Testament underscores the importance of humility in leadership.

> Do nothing out of selfish ambition or vain conceit. Rather, in humility value others above yourselves, not looking to your own interests but each of you to the interests of the others (Philippians 2:3–4, NIV).

This passage advises leaders to consider others as more significant than themselves and to look out for the interests of others. Jesus modeled humility when He washed His disciples' feet, showing that leaders should be willing to serve others and not exalt themselves.

Sacrifice

A servant leader is willing to make personal sacrifices for the sake of others and the greater good. You are not motivated by personal gain but by a desire to make a positive impact and serve the needs of others.

Empowering Others

A servant leader empowers and equips others to reach their full potential. You encourage the growth, development, and success of those you lead, enabling them to thrive and achieve their goals.

Leading by Example

A servant leader leads by example, modeling the values and behaviors you expect from others. You set a positive example through your actions, integrity, and ethical conduct.

> Not lording it over those assigned to your care [do not be arrogant or overbearing], but be examples [of Christian living] to the flock [set a pattern of integrity for your congregation] (1 Peter 5:3, AMP).

Church leaders are encouraged not to lord their authority over others but to be examples to their congregation. Although referring to church leaders, this verse applies to all servant leaders. This principle emphasizes the importance of leaders embodying their values, being role models of faith, and living out what they teach.

Shepherd Leadership

Although shepherds had low status in biblical times, the image of a shepherd is often used to describe leadership. When Jesus was born, angels announced it to shepherds. Jesus called Himself the Good Shepherd.

I am the good shepherd; the good shepherd lays down His life for the sheep. He who is a hired hand, and not a shepherd, who is not the owner of the sheep, sees the wolf coming, and leaves the sheep and flees; and the wolf snatches them and scatters the flock. He flees because he is a hired hand and does not care about the sheep. I am the good shepherd, and I know My own, and My own know Me (John 10:11–14, NASB).

Leaders are encouraged to shepherd and care for their flock, providing guidance, protection, and spiritual nourishment. This concept reflects the idea of leaders leading with love, compassion, and a genuine concern for the well-being of those they lead.

Servant Leadership as a Calling

Servant leadership is not just a leadership style but a calling from God. It is an opportunity to use your position and influence to make a positive impact and serve others as an expression of your faith and commitment to God.

Servant leadership is not about controlling or manipulating others but about selflessly serving and empowering others to reach their full potential. It is a leadership approach that seeks to make a lasting difference by positively impacting the lives of others and glorifying God through acts of service and love.

Christian leadership for kingdom builders is not a position of power and authority but a sacred responsibility. By following Jesus's example, you can embrace the heart of a kingdom builder, lead by example, seek His wisdom, and inspire and mobilize a generation of Christian leaders for God's kingdom. Ignited by a passion for God's kingdom, you lead with a kingdom mindset as the catalysts of transformation and renewal.

4

Christian Leaders in Business

Being a Christian leader in a Kingdom Business means approaching work from a faith-driven and values-centered perspective. This includes having a deep commitment to integrity, honesty, and ethical behavior. As a Christian leader, you primarily seek to reflect the character of Christ in all aspects of your business, especially in interactions with employees, customers, and stakeholders.

Fundamental to a Christian leader is acknowledging that all your success and achievements come from God. It also means being stewards of God's resources in business operations and decision-making, using resources to serve others and glorify God.

Christian business leaders understand the importance of balancing financial success with moral and social responsibilities. This means prioritizing principles such as employee development, community involvement, and environmental sustainability and not solely focusing on profits and financial gain.

As a Christian leader in business, you seek to create a positive impact on society, not just through the quality of your products and services but also by the way you conduct yourself and your business affairs. Your ultimate goal is to honor God and be a witness to His love and grace in the marketplace.

It might be a paradigm shift, but running a highly successful Christian business might mean forgoing profits and financial gain to invest in the well-being of your employees, compensating generously even above market value. Moreover, you've designed your business, so you only work as much as you need to because you have empowered key people, fostering a culture of trust and reliance on capable team members.

Integrating Christian Faith into Business

Integrating Christian faith into business is a common theme among Christian business leaders. Rooted in unwavering principles, five key themes shape a kingdom-driven approach to a profitable business grounded in compassion, service, and integrity.

Faith-Based Leadership

Christian business leaders are encouraged to lead with faith-based values and principles. This may involve prioritizing service, integrity, and ethical decision-making over profit and personal gain.

Biblical Principals in Business

Christian business leaders use the Bible to guide ethical decision-making and business practices. They apply principles from the scripture, such as honesty, fairness, and compassion to business operations, thus, building an ethical and moral foundation for kingdom businesses.

Workplace Ministry

You may also view your business as a ministry, using your platform to share your faith and positively impact employees, customers, and the wider community. This could involve providing employees with spiritual support and resources or using profits to support charitable causes.

Work as Worship

When you view work as worship, all work is seen as a means of serving God. This perspective can help you find greater meaning and purpose in your work and view your business as a way to glorify God.

> Whatever you do, do your work heartily, as for the Lord and not for people, knowing that it is from the Lord that you will receive the reward of the inheritance. It is the Lord Christ whom you serve (Colossians 2:23–24, NASB).

Integrating Christian faith into business means aligning business practices with Christian values and principles. Christian business leaders can build profitable and purposeful businesses rooted in service and compassion principles by prioritizing faith-based leadership, ethical decision-making, and workplace ministry.

Effective Communication

An efficient Christian business leader is empathetic and an expert in communication. A leader communicates the vision, mission, and values effectively and is open to feedback from your team and stakeholders. Communication also involves setting clear expectations and holding people accountable.

It is important to note that communication is a two-way process. You often learn more and make better decisions through direct feedback from others. Although, as a leader, you may excel in generating innovative ideas and vision, you must communicate effectively to rally the support of your leaders and organization behind these ideas for successful implementation.

Leading a discussion is often best when facilitating and allowing others to speak. I learned to talk less and listen more from my years of ministry work as a leader. Now that I am more mature, I have flashbacks of board meetings and times in ministry when I dominated the conversation.

Those who control their tongue will have a long life; opening your mouth can ruin everything (Proverbs 13:3, NLT).

A truly wise person uses few words; a person with understanding is even-tempered. Even fools are thought wise when they keep silent; with their mouths shut, they seem intelligent (Proverbs 17:27–28, NIV).

I have also learned to redirect when a group member dominates the conversation. People are well-intentioned when they find a platform to share, and people listen. But leaders must use tools to keep the ideas moving forward for the whole group. Sometimes you need to put the quiet ones on the spot to hold them accountable and include them in the conversation.

Developing a healthy company culture involves creating a positive work environment that fosters teamwork, accountability, and growth. You prioritize your team's well-being, continuously seek feedback, and offer personal and professional growth opportunities.

Positive Work Environment

From a Christian perspective, cultivating a positive work environment goes beyond mere organizational practices but is rooted in timeless principles found in the Bible. Employees feel valued in a work environment that fosters a sense of dignity, respect, and appreciation.

Lead with Love and Humility

Exhibiting love, kindness, and humility in your interactions with colleagues and employees is- paramount for a Christian business leader. By exemplifying these virtues in your interactions with colleagues and employees, you create an atmosphere of mutual respect and positive relationships. Encouraging employees to treat one another with kindness, understanding, and forgiveness creates a safe and supportive environment where conflicts are resolved biblically.

> Put on then, as God's chosen ones, holy and beloved, compassionate hearts, kindness, humility, meekness, and patience, bearing with one another and, if one has a complaint against another, forgiving each other; as the Lord has forgiven you, so you also must forgive. And above all these put on love, which binds everything together in perfect harmony (Colossians 3:12–14, ESV).

Practice Forgiveness

Forgiveness is a fundamental Christian principle. Encourage forgiveness among team members when conflicts or misunderstandings arise. Promote open and honest communication to resolve issues and prevent grudges from lingering.

> For if you forgive other people for their offenses, your heavenly Father will also forgive you (Matthew 6:14, NASB).

Emphasize Integrity and Ethical Behavior

Encourage employees to adhere to high honesty, integrity, and ethical standards. In such an environment, people feel accountable for their actions and are empowered to do what is right, even when no one is watching.

> He grants a treasure of common sense to the honest. He is a shield to those who walk with integrity. He guards the paths of the just and protects those who are faithful to him (Proverbs 2:7–8, NLT).

Foster Teamwork and Collaboration

Fostering collaboration and teamwork among colleagues is another critical aspect of a positive work environment. Highlight the value of everyone's contribution and create opportunities for team-building exercises, joint projects, and cross-departmental interactions. Adopt a workplace culture that values open and honest communication, welcoming feedback, suggestions, and concerns with humility, grace, and respect.

> Yes, there are many parts, but only one body. The eye can never say to the hand, "I don't need you." The head can't say to the feet, "I don't need you." In fact, some parts of the body that seem weakest and least important are actually the most necessary. And the parts we regard as less honorable are those we clothe with the greatest care. So we carefully protect those parts that should not be seen, while the more honorable parts do not require this special care. So God has put the body together such that extra honor and care are given to those parts that have less dignity. This makes for harmony among the members, so that all the members care for each other (1 Corinthians 12:20–25, NLT).

Support Work-Life Balance

Prioritize the well-being of employees, both inside and outside of the workplace. By offering flexible work arrangements, resources for stress management, and honoring personal commitments, you promote a healthy work-life balance that respects the importance of family, personal well-being, and spiritual growth. Encourage employees to balance work commitments with their faith, relationships, and self-care.

> The Lord directs the steps of the godly. He delights in every detail of their lives. Though they stumble, they will never fall, for the Lord holds them by the hand (Psalm 37:23–24, NLT).

Promote Personal Growth and Development

Provide opportunities for employees to grow personally and professionally. Invest in developing your employees with training programs, mentorship, and educational resources that align with Christian values. Support employees in their career aspirations, encourage them to pursue lifelong learning, and use their talents and abilities to serve others.

> Practice and cultivate and meditate upon these duties; throw yourself wholly into them [as your ministry], so that your progress may be evident to everybody (1 Timothy 4:15, AMPC).

> Then the way you live will always honor and please the Lord, and your lives will produce every kind of good fruit. All the while, you will grow as you learn to know God better and better (Colossians 1:10, NLT).

Culture of Gratitude and Appreciation

Celebrate and recognize achievements, milestones, and personal growth. Encourage employees to acknowledge and support one another's accomplishments. Express gratitude and appreciation for the contributions of individuals and teams' hard work and dedication with public acknowledgments, rewards, or appreciation events.

> Therefore encourage (admonish, exhort) one another and edify (strengthen and build up) one another, just as you are doing. Now also we beseech you, brethren, get to know those who labor among you [recognize them for what they are, acknowledge and appreciate and respect them all]—your leaders who are over you in the Lord and those who warn and kindly reprove and exhort you. And hold them in very high and most affectionate esteem in [intelligent and sympathetic] appreciation of their work. Be at peace among yourselves (1 Thessalonians 5:11–13, AMPC).

Practice Servant Leadership

Adopt a servant leadership mindset, exemplifying Jesus's teachings on serving others. Prioritize the well-being and development of your team members and support their growth. Lead by serving your employees, listening to their needs, and empowering them to reach their full potential. Be humble, compassionate, and willing to put their needs above yours.

> But it is not this way for you; rather, the one who is the greatest among you must become like the youngest, and the leader like the servant (Luke 22:26, NASB).

Encourage Acts of Service and Volunteering

Promote and support employee participation in community service initiatives, charity work, and volunteering opportunities. Support the practice of Christ's teachings to love and serve others by actively engaging in acts of service together as an organization.

> Little children, let's not love with word or with tongue, but in deed and truth (1 John 3:18, NASB).

> As each one has received a special gift, employ it in serving one another as good stewards of the multifaceted grace of God (1 Peter 4:10, NASB).

Create Opportunities for Spiritual Growth

Recognize and support the spiritual aspect of individuals' lives. Provide opportunities for prayer, Bible study, and fellowship within the workplace, respecting the diversity of employees' faith perspectives while nurturing a spiritual environment.

> But grow in the grace and knowledge of our Lord and Savior Jesus Christ. To Him be the glory both now and forever (2 Peter 3:18, NKJV).

Seek God's Guidance

Above all, seek God's guidance and wisdom through prayer. Ask Him for wisdom in decision-making, resolving conflicts, and creating a positive work environment. Trust in His providence and believe that He will help you in your efforts.

> The Lord will guide you continually, and satisfy your soul in drought, and strengthen your bones; you shall be like a watered garden, and like a spring of water, whose waters do not fail (Isaiah 58:11, NKJV).

Integrating these Christian principles into the workplace can create a positive work environment where employees feel valued, respected, and supported, aligning with Christian principles of love, service, and humility.

Retaining Top Talent

Attracting and retaining top talent is crucial for long-term success. From a Christian perspective, drawing exceptional team members in business involves incorporating principles and values from the Bible into your recruitment strategy.

Demonstrate a Values-Driven Culture

Communicate and emphasize the Christian values that guide your organization. Highlight principles such as integrity, honesty, and servant leadership. Prospective employees who share these values are more likely to be attracted to your company.

Model Ethical Behavior

As a business leader, consistently demonstrate ethical behavior and decision-making rooted in Christian values. By prioritizing moral conduct and operating with a higher purpose beyond profit, your kingdom business will appeal to like-minded individuals who share the same values

Prioritize Employee Well-Being

Show genuine concern for the well-being of your employees by offering competitive compensation, benefits, and a healthy work-life balance. Promote a positive and supportive work environment that nurtures personal and professional growth, fostering loyalty and commitment among the team.

Highlight Opportunities for Servant Leadership

Promote a culture of servant leadership, where leaders prioritize serving and supporting their teams. Prospective employees are often attracted to organizations that encourage leadership styles that align with Christian teachings.

Foster a Collaborative and Inclusive Environment

Create an environment that values collaboration, teamwork, and inclusivity. Encourage diverse perspectives and treat everyone with respect and dignity. Prospective employees are more likely to be drawn to organizations that embrace inclusivity and foster a sense of belonging.

Emphasize Purpose and Meaning

Highlight the mission and purpose of your organization, demonstrating how it aligns with Christian values. Articulate how your business positively impacts society and how potential employees can contribute to that mission.

Engage in Community and Social Initiatives

Engage in community outreach and social initiatives that align with Christian teachings. Prospective employees often seek meaningful companies that actively give back to the community and make a positive difference.

Encourage Faith Expression

Acknowledge and accommodate employees' faith expression by providing opportunities for prayer, spiritual reflection, or workplace fellowship groups. Respect the diversity of faith perspectives while nurturing a supportive spiritual environment.

Leverage Personal Networks and Referrals

Tap into personal networks and referrals within Christian communities. Network with faith-based organizations or partner with Christian job boards or community groups to reach top talent aligned with your values.

Seek God's Guidance

Pray for guidance and discernment in attracting the right individuals to your organization. Trust that God will lead you to the talented individuals who share your values and are best suited for your business.

By aligning your recruitment strategy with Christian principles, you can attract top talent who are not only highly skilled but also share your organization's values, leading to a more harmonious and kingdom-driven workplace.

Taking Calculated Chances

Another area of a Kingdom Builder's stewardship of a business is the willingness to take calculated chances and step out in faith. Always consult your circle of influence and team before making irrational or emotional decisions. Growth often requires venturing beyond the familiar, exploring new approaches, and making well-thought-out decisions while planning for the possibility of failure. A Spirit-filled green light for a business decision doesn't mean it will work perfectly the first time; there may be a learning curve and setbacks along the way. Failures are valuable learning opportunities that contribute to the dynamic success of your Kingdom Business over time.

"If you are not willing to risk the unusual, you will have to settle for the ordinary."—Rick Warren

This insightful quote emphasizes the importance of taking risks and stepping outside of your comfort zone to achieve greatness. Embracing failure is part of the learning process is essential. Setbacks should not deter you but rather strengthen your resolve to persevere and learn from experience …

"Failure is never final unless you give up."—Rick Warren

This quote encourages people to persevere and not let setbacks define them. It highlights the importance of resilience and the mindset of not giving up.

Overall, a kingdom builder's philosophy on failure is one of embracing risk-taking and the invaluable learning opportunities that accompany failure. You can achieve your goals and reach your full potential by taking chances and not fearing failure. These principles guide your kingdom-building approach to embracing calculated risks.

Embracing Risks

A kingdom builder should be open to taking calculated risks and stepping out in faith. Growth and progress often require stepping outside of your comfort zone and being willing to try new approaches or strategies.

RYAN BOURQUE, CPA, MBT, CKA

Learning from Setbacks

Failure is a natural part of any endeavor, including ministry. Embrace failures and setbacks as opportunities for growth and refinement. Evaluate what went wrong, make necessary adjustments, and move forward with resilience and renewed wisdom.

Staying True to Purpose

Stay focused on the organization's core purpose and vision, even in the face of setbacks. You should align decisions with the overarching mission and values, ensuring that you remain committed to the larger purpose you are called to fulfill, even if specific ventures fail.

Accountability and Evaluation

Implement systems of accountability and evaluation to assess the success or failure of decisions. Regularly review and reflect on the outcomes of decisions to gain valuable insights and guide future choices.

Foster a Culture of Innovation

Cultivate an organizational culture that encourages innovative thinking and rewards calculated risks. Create an environment where team members feel empowered to explore new ideas and approaches.

Encourage a Growth Mindset

Promote a growth mindset among your team, where failures are viewed as opportunities for learning and improvement. Encourage continuous learning and a willingness to embrace challenges.

Trust God's Providence

Ultimately, trust in God's providence and plan for your business. Seek His guidance and rely on His promises, knowing He is in control and will work all things together for good.

Employee Performance Evaluation

From a biblical perspective, evaluating an employee's performance involves aligning it with the principles and values found in scripture.

> But the fruit of the Spirit [the result of His presence within us] is love [unselfish concern for others], joy, [inner] peace, patience [not the ability to wait, but how we act while waiting], kindness, goodness, faithfulness, gentleness, self-control. Against such things there is no law (Galatians 5:22–23, AMP).

This passage is part of a more extensive discussion on living in the Spirit versus living according to the flesh. The apostle Paul, the author of Galatians, describes how those who walk by the Spirit exhibit certain characteristics or fruits that reflect their relationship with God.

Character and Fruit of the Spirit

Evaluate the employee's character and whether they display the fruit of the Spirit, as outlined in Galatians 5:22–23. Do they exhibit these qualities in their interactions and conduct?

The fruits of the Spirit are qualities and virtues that believers should strive to cultivate in their lives through the help of the Holy Spirit. It helps individuals develop a Christ-like character and contributes to healthy relationships, personal growth, and overall well-being.

Love

The unconditional and sacrificial love for God and others, it seeks the well-being of others above your own.

> Jesus replied, "You must love the Lord your God with all your heart, all your soul, and all your mind. This is the first and greatest commandment. A second is equally important: Love your neighbor as yourself. The entire law and all the demands of the prophets are based on these two commandments" (Matthew 22:37–40, NLT).

Joy

The joy of the Lord is a deep and lasting inner gladness based on hope and assurance in God. It's not a pursuit of happiness but being joyous in all circumstances.

> Then he said to them, "Go your way, eat the fat, drink the sweet, and send portions to those for whom nothing is prepared; for this day is holy to our Lord. Do not sorrow, for the joy of the Lord is your strength," (Nehemiah 8:10, NKJV).

Peace

Having God's peace is harmony, tranquility, and a sense of wholeness in your relationship with God and others.

> Peace I leave with you; My [perfect] peace I give to you; not as the world gives do I give to you. Do not let your heart be troubled, nor let it be afraid. [Let My perfect peace calm you in every circumstance and give you courage and strength for every challenge] (John 14:27, AMP).

Patience (Longsuffering)

Longsuffering is the ability to endure, persevere, and show patience in challenging circumstances or with difficult people.

> [Living as becomes you] with complete lowliness of mind (humility) and meekness (unselfishness, gentleness, mildness), with patience, bearing with one another and making allowances because you love one another (Ephesians 4:2, AMPC).

Kindness

Kindness is a generous and considerate attitude, showing empathy and compassion toward others.

> Be kind to one another, compassionate, forgiving each other, just as God in Christ also has forgiven you (Ephesians 4:32, NASB).

Goodness

Goodness is moral excellence, integrity, and virtue in thoughts, words, and deeds.

> Surely your goodness and love will follow me all the days of my life, and I will dwell in the house of the Lord forever (Psalm 23:6, NIV).

Faithfulness

Faithfulness means being trustworthy, reliable, and loyal in keeping commitments and relationships.

> And the Lord said, "Who then is that faithful and wise steward, whom his master will make ruler over his

household, to give them their portion of food in due season?" (Luke 12:42, NKJV).

Gentleness

Gentleness means humility, meekness, and a controlled strength in interactions with others.

Let your gentle spirit be known to all people. The Lord is near (Philippians 4:5, NASB).

Self-Control

Self-control is discipline and mastery over your desires, emotions, and actions.

For the grace of God has appeared, bringing salvation for all people, training us to renounce ungodliness and worldly passions, and to live self-controlled, upright, and godly lives in the present age, waiting for our blessed hope, the appearing of the glory of our great God and Savior Jesus Christ, who gave himself for us to redeem us from all lawlessness and to purify for himself a people for his own possession who are zealous for good works (Titus 2:11–14, ESV).

These fruits reflect the character of Christ and are to be cultivated and demonstrated by believers as evidence of a transformed life in the Spirit. They guide believers toward a life of love, service, and righteousness, reflecting God's nature and bringing glory to Him.

The Fruit of the Holy Spirit is an excellent way to assess an employee's performance. Leading by example will encourage your employees to do likewise. You can measure these qualities and behaviors in your employees using the following criteria.

Honesty and Integrity

Assess the employee's honesty and integrity in their work and whether they consistently adhere to biblical principles of truthfulness, trustworthiness, and ethical conduct.

Faithfulness and Diligence

Evaluate the employee's faithfulness and diligence in carrying out their responsibilities. Are they committed to their work, doing it to the best of their abilities, and fulfilling their duties with a spirit of excellence?

Stewardship

Assess how well the employee manages the resources and responsibilities entrusted to them. Are they utilizing time, talents, and resources effectively and responsibly for the greater good of the organization and others?

Servant Leadership

Evaluate the employee's willingness to serve and support others within the organization and the broader community. Do they demonstrate a humble and selfless attitude, exemplifying Christ's servant leadership?

Collaboration and Teamwork

Assess the employee's ability to work well with others, fostering a spirit of unity, cooperation, and respect in team settings. Are they contributing positively to a harmonious work environment?

Continuous Growth and Learning

Assess the employee's commitment to personal and professional growth and willingness to learn, adapt, and develop new skills. Are they actively seeking to improve themselves and contribute to improving the organization?

Impact and Contribution

Evaluate the employee's overall impact and contribution to the organization, their role in promoting its mission, vision, and values, and their positive influence on colleagues and stakeholders.

It's important to note that performance evaluation should be approached with grace, mercy, and fairness, recognizing that all employees have different strengths, weaknesses, and growth areas. The goal is to encourage growth, provide constructive feedback, and support employees on their journey toward becoming more Christ-like in their work and relationships.

5

Kingdom Builder Business Concept

Recently, a transformation occurred in the business world, where kingdom businesses are shifting their focus from being solely profit-driven to embracing a kingdom purpose. A kingdom builder's business is a company that aligns its mission, values, and operations with a greater sense of purpose. This sense of purpose goes beyond generating profits and aims to contribute positively to society.

Purpose-Driven vs. Profit-Driven Business

A purpose-driven business is founded on five core principles: worship, ministry, evangelism, fellowship, and discipleship. Each of these principles is based on the teachings of Jesus Christ and is designed to help a business fulfill its more significant purpose.

The first principle of worship involves prioritizing God first and seeking to serve others, whether they are employees, customers, or stakeholders. Ministry is the second principle—using the business as a platform to help those in need and positively impact society. Evangelism, the third principle, entails communicating the company's values, mission, and purpose to employees and customers. Fellowship, the fourth principle, emphasizes creating a sense of community and connection among staff and customers. Lastly, discipleship focuses on providing opportunities for personal growth and development for employees and customers.

The advantage of a purpose-driven business over a solely profit-driven company is attracting and retaining highly motivated employees dedicated to the company's mission and values. This leads to increased employee engagement, job satisfaction, and overall productivity. A purpose-driven business excels at building and maintaining strong customer relationships, and fostering long-term customer loyalty and brand recognition by aligning your mission and values with customers' needs and wants.

Another advantage is the positive impact a purpose-driven business it has on communities as it leverages resources, networks, and platforms to contribute to society. Your company earns the respect and admiration of its stakeholders, enhancing your corporate image and attracting investors and partners who share your social and environmental values.

The concept of purpose-driven business has gained significant traction, not just a trend but a lasting movement. By aligning your mission, values, and operations with a greater sense of purpose, your business can capture the hearts and minds of your employees, customers, and stakeholders. By embracing the principles outlined in *The Purpose Driven Church* and *The Purpose Driven Life*, companies can become purpose-driven enterprises that make a difference in the world.

What Sets a Kingdom Builder's Business Apart?

Being a kingdom builder's business transcends traditional entrepreneurship with the explicit purpose and intention of advancing the kingdom of God. You align your business practices, decisions, and impact with the values and principles of the kingdom.

Kingdom-Focused Vision

A kingdom builder's business has a vision that goes beyond profit and success. It seeks to make a positive and lasting impact by aligning its goals and strategies with God's purposes and priorities.

Ethical and Moral Integrity

A kingdom builder prioritizes ethical conduct and integrity in all business operations. You seek to uphold biblical principles of honesty, fairness, transparency, and accountability.

Servant Leadership

A kingdom builder has a servant leadership mindset, recognizing that leadership is about serving and empowering others. You lead with humility, compassion, and a genuine desire to impact the lives of employees, customers, and others you interact with.

People-First Approach

A kingdom builder prioritizes the well-being and growth of your employees at the forefront, valuing them as individuals and investing in their development. You create a healthy work environment that fosters personal and professional growth, values diversity and inclusion, and treats employees with dignity and respect.

Purpose-Driven Business

A kingdom builder's business operates with a higher purpose beyond financial gain. It seeks to address societal needs, contribute positively to communities, and use its resources to make a difference.

Kingdom Values in Decision-Making

A kingdom builder makes business decisions based on biblical values and principles, seeking guidance from God, His Word, and the Holy Spirit. In your decision-making processes, you weigh the impact of your choices on all stakeholders and consider the greater good.

Impact and Influence

A kingdom builder's business actively seeks opportunities to positively impact society and influence its industry. It exercises influence to advocate for justice, compassion, stewardship of resources, and sustainable practices.

Kingdom Collaboration

Recognizing that building the kingdom of God is not a solitary endeavor, you actively collaborate with like-minded individuals, organizations, and churches. You seek partnerships and alliances that amplify the impact and promote shared kingdom goals.

Ultimately, being a kingdom builder business means using your business as a platform to advance God's kingdom, making a difference in the lives of people, communities, and society. It involves integrating faith and business, pursuing excellence, and seeking to honor God in all aspects of your operations.

Ways Kingdom Builder Businesses Collaborate

Collaboration among Christian businesses can be a powerful way to advance God's kingdom, strengthen missions, and amplify the impact of individual enterprises. Here are some lesser-known ways to collaborate with each other.

Joint Marketing Initiatives

Partner with other Christian businesses in complementary industries to create joint marketing campaigns. Co-host events, cross-promoting products or services, or pooling resources for marketing materials. By collaborating and leveraging each other's networks and customer bases, you can expand your reach and introduce products and services to new audiences.

Mentoring and Coaching

Mentoring and coaching are powerful tools for personal and spiritual growth opportunities, sharing wisdom and experience, and leaving a lasting legacy. Both parties benefit from the experience. The mentor establishes a personal relationship with the mentee by investing time and energy. A good mentor guides and supports the mentee with patience and humility, positively impacting the mentee.

As a Christian, you should guide and disciple others by your lifestyle, sharing your faith, and leading by example. Seek opportunities to mentor and share your experiences; everyone has something valuable to share.

Establish mentoring or coaching programs where experienced Christian business owners or executives can guide and support startups or smaller businesses. This collaboration can involve sharing knowledge, giving advice, and fostering a community of learning and growth among Christian entrepreneurs. You can also establish formal mentoring programs within a Christian business network.

Supplier and Vendor Networks

Build networks with other Christian-owned suppliers and vendors to enhance the ethical and sustainable practices within your supply chains. You can source products or services from each other, support fair trade practices, or share information on sustainable sourcing options. By prioritizing business with other Christian companies when feasible, you create a partnership that supports and strengthens fellow Christian businesses while promoting shared values and principles.

Resource Sharing

Kingdom builder businesses and ministries are designed to collaborate in sharing resources such as office spaces, equipment, or expertise. Pooling resources, knowledge, and skills can reduce costs, improve efficiency, give access to specialized expertise, and provide access to resources that might otherwise be unaffordable for individual businesses. By sharing resources, you can create a supportive ecosystem of Christian businesses that mutually benefit and thrive.

Strategic Partnerships

Explore strategic partnerships with other kingdom builders and Christian businesses that align with your mission, values, and target audience. Joint ventures, product collaborations, or co-developing projects can achieve mutual impact and beneficial outcomes.

Prayer Networks

Create a culture of prayer and support within the kingdom builders' community. Offer support, encouragement, and resources when needed, fostering a sense of unity and collaboration based on the early church model.

Establish prayer networks or groups for Christian business owners to regularly pray for each other's businesses, challenges, and opportunities. These prayer networks can provide spiritual support, encouragement, and a sense of unity and accountability within the community.

> They devoted themselves to the apostles' teaching and to fellowship, to the breaking of bread and to prayer. Everyone was filled with awe at the many wonders and signs performed by the apostles. All the believers were together

and had everything in common. They sold property and possessions to give to anyone who had need. Every day they continued to meet together in the temple courts. They broke bread in their homes and ate together with glad and sincere hearts, praising God and enjoying the favor of all the people. And the Lord added to their number daily those who were being saved (Acts 2:42–47, NIV).

Collaboration for Social Impact

Partner with other Christian businesses to tackle social issues and collectively impact the community. Collaborate on charitable initiatives, support local causes, or work together to address societal needs. You can maximize your efforts and create a lasting impact by pooling resources and expertise.

Business Conferences and Events

Attend or organize Christian business conferences, seminars, or events where business owners can share knowledge, insights, and experiences. This fosters networking, learning, and the opportunity to build relationships with like-minded individuals. Consider hosting panels, workshops, or collaborative sessions during these events to encourage collaboration and knowledge sharing.

Online Forums and Communities

Join or create online forums or communities specifically for Christian business owners. These platforms can provide a space for sharing ideas, seeking advice, and collaborating on specific projects. Engage in discussions, ask questions, and explore potential partnerships with other community members.

Collaboration can foster unity, support, and collective impact among Christian businesses. Approach collaboration with humility and a servant's heart, seeking mutual benefit while honoring God's principles and values. Kingdom builder business owners can unite and leverage each other's strengths to reinforce shared missions of advancing God's kingdom through collective efforts.

ESG from a Christian Perspective

Implementing Environmental, Social, and Governance (ESG) practices from a Christian perspective involves aligning these practices with biblical principles and values. You have a sacred responsibility to be a good steward of God's kingdom. Consider these general guidelines when incorporating ESG into business or investment decisions.

Environmental Stewardship

God created the earth and commanded mankind to protect and preserve it as good stewards. Responsible environmental practices seek to honor God's creation. This means minimizing negative environmental impacts, conserving resources, supporting sustainable practices, and considering the long-term effects of business activities.

Social Responsibility

Prioritize the well-being, dignity, and fair treatment of all stakeholders, including employees, customers, suppliers, and communities. Embrace the call to love your neighbor as yourself and ensure just and equitable practices within the organization and broader society.

Ethical Governance

Promote integrity, transparency, accountability, and ethical behavior principles in decision-making. Follow biblical principles of justice and fairness, avoiding corruption, dishonesty, and exploitation.

Biblical Values and Screening

Incorporate biblical values and ethical screens into investment decisions, ensuring alignment with Christian beliefs. This may involve avoiding investments in industries or businesses that conflict with biblical principles, such as those involved in pornography, gambling, or harmful products.

Engaging with Companies

Engage with companies or organizations to advocate for positive change, encouraging them to adopt ESG practices that align with biblical values. Use influence, dialogue, and constructive engagement to promote positive transformation within the organization and the wider industry.

Impact Investing

Consider investments that intentionally seek positive social or environmental impacts alongside financial returns. This may involve supporting companies or initiatives that address societal challenges, promote sustainable practices, or contribute to the well-being of communities.

Responsible Stewardship of Resources

Make intentional choices in allocating and using financial resources to support ESG initiatives or invest in companies prioritizing ESG practices. Seek wisdom and discernment to ensure that resources are used in a way that honors God and advances His kingdom.

Seeking God's Guidance

Studying and understanding the scriptures is crucial, as well as seeking guidance from the Holy Spirit and involving like-minded Christian advisors or organizations when implementing ESG practices from a Christian perspective. Remember, your ultimate goal is to reflect Christ's values, using resources to honor God, serve others, and advance His kingdom.

By embracing ESG practices through a Christian lens, you aim to fulfill your divine calling to be faithful stewards and positively impact your surroundings.

Christian Business and AI

Artificial intelligence (AI) is undoubtedly transforming industries and businesses globally, including those rooted in Christian faith and principles. Christian business leaders must navigate the challenges and opportunities presented by AI to serve customers, employees, and stakeholders effectively.

From a Christian perspective, AI can be seen as a tool humans create to serve the greater good, just as all technologies are. It is neither inherently good nor evil, but how it is used determines its impact. As such, Christian business leaders must adopt a holistic approach to using AI, balancing the potential benefits and risks with Christian ethics and values. Consider these critical points when integrating AI into your kingdom builder business.

Honoring Human Dignity

Christianity highly values human life and dignity—souls are precious to the Lord. AI can automate tasks and improve efficiency, but it should not be used to replace human workers or treat them as expendable. Christian business leaders must ensure that AI does not undermine the dignity and value of human work and workers but rather should complement human capabilities and enhance their roles as God's creation.

Ensuring Transparency and Accountability

As AI starts to make decisions and carry out tasks, it's crucial to maintain transparency in your decision-making and be accountable for your actions.

This includes ensuring that algorithms are free of bias and that ethical considerations are considered when developing and implementing AI.

Fostering Human Creativity

AI can excel at repetitive and routine tasks but cannot replace human creativity and imagination from God. Christian business leaders must ensure that AI enhances rather than replaces human creativity. Moreover, it would help if you encouraged employees to use AI to free up time for more creative endeavors, such as brainstorming or ideation.

Promoting Social Good

As a Christian, you are called to love your neighbors as yourselves and to work for the common good. AI can address complex social problems like poverty, inequality, and injustice. Christian business leaders should look for ways to use AI to promote social good and advance God's kingdom.

Biased AI System

While AI has its strengths, it's not all-powerful and has limitations, and depending on the input, bias can occur. Bias in AI systems refers to unfair or discriminatory outcomes resulting from the data used to train the AI model or the design decisions made during its development. AI models learn from vast amounts of data. Suppose that data contains biases or reflects existing societal prejudices. In that case, the AI system can inadvertently perpetuate and amplify those biases in its decision-making process.

No Savior or Holy Spirit

Artificial intelligence may offer applicable Bible passages and seem to provide great teachings, like the religious leaders in the Old Testament who had the head knowledge but didn't know the Savior. AI isn't human. AI doesn't have a soul, it cannot accept Jesus as its Savior or have the

Holy Spirit living inside to provide revelatory knowledge and guide it in God's way.

As a Christian business leader, you must grapple with the ethical implications of AI as you seek to serve the Lord and others. By honoring human dignity, ensuring transparency and accountability, fostering human creativity, and promoting social good, you can leverage the potential of AI to create a better future for all.

Kingdom Builder Businesses Give Back

As a Christian, running a business goes beyond just making a profit; it includes contributing positively to the community by giving back. Your faith motivates you to give to those in need, serve others, and show God's love to your community. Giving back enables you to fuel your evangelism efforts, create a lasting impact on the community, and promote your business with a purposeful heart.

Giving Back to the Community

Giving back to the community should be integral to every kingdom builder's business. It promotes kindness, compassion, and empathy—qualities distinguishing Christians from the rest of society. Whether volunteering, donating to charity organizations, or sponsoring community events, giving back should inspire others and radiate God's love throughout the community. To give back effectively, identify your community's specific needs and collaborate with organizations already impacting communities. This will enable the business to determine which initiative to support, what resources to allocate, and how to approach the people to reach the intended recipients.

Impact of Giving Back on Evangelism

As a Christian, you are called to evangelize and to spread the love and teachings of Jesus Christ to others. Giving back enables you to accomplish this in a meaningful way. People often hesitate to listen to the gospel because the Christian community does not resonate with them. Therefore, giving back serves as an evangelism tool by creating a positive impact and allowing you to share your faith with others.

When a Christian business gives back to the community, it builds trust and credibility, and people become more receptive to the gospel. Giving back also helps to break down barriers and build relationships with the community. Your actions become a tangible representation of Christ's love, breaking down barriers and building relationships with the community.

Examples of Giving Back by Christian Businesses

Christian businesses can give back to the community in many ways. Some companies organize charity events, support local charities, sponsor community sports teams, and offer mentorship programs. Others donate some of their profit to charity organizations or partner with nonprofit organizations to provide financial and logistical support. Still, others give underprivileged youth a scholarship for education or job training.

> One great example is Chick-fil-A. The fast-food franchise is renowned for being generous while adhering to Christian principles. Chick-fil-A has donated millions of dollars to charity organizations, and their franchises often participate in local charity events, like donating meals to essential workers or paying for customers' meals. Their philanthropy has not only attracted loyal customers but has also helped to spread the gospel of love and compassion.

> "We all have a steward's heart. It's not ours, but everything we have is on loan to us from God."—David Green

Billionaire David Green, the visionary founder of Hobby Lobby, is a living testament to the principles of stewardship. In his book, *More Than a Hobby*, he shares the transformative journey of practicing stewardship of affluence and influence through the success of Hobby Lobby arts and craft stores. Beyond business success, David Green's heart for serving God and others is evident in his generous contributions to the advancement of the gospel and the establishment of the Museum of the Bible in Washington, DC. His unwavering belief that Christians are mere managers of possession and wealth, responsible for utilizing these resources for God's purpose, reflects a profound commitment to kingdom building.

An excellent example of David Green's dedication to stewardship can be seen in his involvement with the Garden Growth Community Church, also known as Reverend Schuller/Crystal Cathedral. When the church was selling its retreat property in San Juan Capistrano, Saddleback Church expressed interest in buying it, even without the budget. When Pastor Rick reached out to David Green for assistance with children's items for the church's anniversary event at Angels Stadium, he received the response that Hobby Lobby's mission focused primarily on other endeavors.

In a display of God's divine providence, David Green later took the initiative to purchase the San Juan Capistrano retreat property and graciously leased it to Saddleback Church for a symbolic $1. Despite the property's state of disrepair and deferred maintenance—I know this because I served there, helping fix the property—David's act of stewardship demonstrated his deep understanding of God's divine plan.

After a period of responsible care and thoughtful management, David Green eventually donated the property to Saddleback Church. This act of generosity allowed the church to make the best use of the property in its efforts to expand the kingdom, reaching more followers of Christ through additional campuses. David Green's life serves as an extraordinary example of integrating the stewardship of influence and affluence. When your influence and wealth align with God's purpose for your life, you can contribute to His redemptive work in the world. It's an intentional lifestyle where your choices reflect your commitment to stewardship. You stay on course by establishing accountability structures and regularly reflecting on whether you utilize your influence and affluence to honor God.

Giving back to your community is an essential part of your Christian faith. It allows you to radiate God's love, kindness, and compassion, spreading the gospel through meaningful actions. Through your giving, you become the hands and feet of Christ, extending God's love to the community and winning souls into the kingdom.

6

Journey of Significance— Redefining Success

The journey of significance represents the transition from being accomplished to leaving a lasting and eternal impact perpetuated beyond your career and lifetime. Transitioning from success to significance is a deeply personal journey that varies for each individual.

In my early twenties, I achieved success through co-managing a tax practice, instructing at UC Irvine DCE, teaching in ministry, and running a thriving consumer technology startup. I remember running the math and projections on my future income and investments from saving more than half of my income. My financial projections were promising, leading me to question the purpose of pursuing even greater success. Despite my proportional giving, I had yet to embrace a generosity mindset fully. During that period, I made many friends through a private member-only club and from my community in Newport Coast, California, a very affluent neighborhood filled with successful well-educated, driven people.

The notion that "It's lonely at the to"" resonated with me, knowing leaders and successful individuals often feel isolated. Through my work with pastors as a CPA, I discovered that they, too, experience feelings of isolation and loneliness. However, I realized that living a life of significance, guided by a Christian perspective, involves intentionally using my talents and resources to serve others and make a positive impact. Transitioning from a self-centered pursuit of success to a life of significance aligned with God's purposes requires embracing practical steps. These key components will help you uncover the beauty of living a life marked by purpose, impact, and eternal value.

Seeking God's Will

Significance from a kingdom builder's viewpoint entails living in alignment with God's purpose and centering on fulfilling His will. It's glorifying Him through your actions. It is not primarily about personal achievement or fame but about living a life pleasing to God and fulfilling His plan for you.

"For I know the plans that I have for you, declares the Lord, plans for prosperity and not for disaster, to give you a future and a hope" (Jeremiah 29:11, NASB). As a kingdom builder, your life only has an impact when you prioritize prayer, seeking God's guidance, and spending intentional time in His presence. Gain wisdom and insight from God's Word to discern His purposes for your life.

Surrendering your plans is when you learn to submit your desires and ambitions to God's sovereignty and seek His will above all. It involves recognizing that your worth and purpose come from being loved and redeemed by God through Jesus Christ.

> Commit to the Lord whatever you do, and he will establish your plans (Proverbs 16:3, NIV).

> We can make our plans, but the Lord determines our steps (Proverbs 16:9, NLT).

Shifting to Servant Leadership

True significance is found in emulating Jesus's example of love and service to others, embracing and using the gifts, talents, and resources that God has given you to make a positive difference in the world, whether through acts of kindness, compassion, justice, or sharing the message of God's love.

The heart of a servant leader is embracing a Christ-like attitude of humility, compassion, and selflessness in your interactions with others. The power of servant leadership is that success is measured by your positive impact on those you lead. By nurturing a culture of service, you create an environment where service is celebrated and the needs of others are prioritized.

> So Jesus called them together and said, "You know that the rulers in this world lord it over their people, and officials flaunt their authority over those under them. But among you it will be different. Whoever wants to be a leader among you must be your servant, and whoever wants to be first among you must be the slave of everyone else," (Mark 10:42–44, NLT).

Cultivating Generosity

The joy of giving is recognizing that true significance lies in generous giving and sharing your time, resources, and talents with others.

> I have shown you in every way, by laboring like this, that you must support the weak. And remember the words of the Lord Jesus, that He said, "It is more blessed to give than to receive" (Acts 20:35, NKJV).

Wise stewardship is understanding that all you have is entrusted to you by God and learning to manage your resources in ways that honor Him. Support causes that align with God's heart and invest in initiatives with eternal significance.

Making Kingdom Impact a Priority

Significance is intertwined with eternal values and actions that have lasting impact and significance in light of eternity. Collaborating with like-minded individuals and organizations to maximize your collective impact on God's kingdom. By shifting your perspective from temporary success to eternal impact, you are focusing on building God's kingdom. Discerning how your unique skills, experiences, and resources can be used to further God's purposes will present new opportunities.

Nurturing Relationships

As a kingdom builder, it's important to nurture vertical and horizontal relationships and invest in the future of the next generation. Your vertical relationship is when you deepen your connection with God, making Him the center of your life and seeking intimacy through prayer, worship, and obedience. Horizontal relationships recognize the value of healthy and meaningful connections with others, cultivating love, empathy, and encouragement in your interactions. Invest in the next generation with mentoring, discipleship, and passing on the baton of faith to equip the younger generation for a life of significance.

> Love the Lord your God with all your heart and with all your soul and with all your mind and with all your strength. The second is this: Love your neighbor as yourself. There is no commandment greater than these (Mark 12:30–31, NIV).

Living with Integrity and Character

Align with God's truth. Embrace biblical principles as the foundation for your decisions, actions, and relationships.

> But when he, the Spirit of truth, comes, he will guide you into all the truth. He will not speak on his own; he will speak only what he hears, and he will tell you what is yet to come (John 16:13, NIV).

Honor God in all spheres by integrating your faith into every aspect of your life, whether in the workplace, family, or community. Walk in integrity. Cultivate a reputation of trustworthiness, honesty, and moral uprightness that reflects the character of Christ.

By seeking God's will, embracing servant leadership, practicing generosity, prioritizing kingdom impact, nurturing relationships, and living with integrity, you can experience the true fulfillment of aligning your lives with God's purposes.

May you embark on this transformative journey, where success is redefined and significance is found in surrendering to God's divine plan for your life.

Overall, significance in Christ is about aligning your life with God's purpose, glorifying Him through faithful living, and positively impacting others through acts of love, service, and sharing the message of salvation. It is living a life of purpose, guided by biblical principles and empowered by the Holy Spirit.

Transformative Journey Steps

These steps serve as a general for transitioning journey, recognizing that each person's journey is unique and may vary. These steps are a general framework; it's important to listen to your intuition, seek God's guidance, and adapt to your circumstances and values.

Reflect and Examine

Reflect on your current definition of success and examine whether it aligns with biblical values, passions, and purpose. Explore what its significance means to you and why you desire it.

Identify Your Values and Purpose

Seek to understand your core values, the principles that guide your life, and the purpose you believe you were created for. Consider how these values and purpose can shape your pursuit of significance.

Clarify Your Vision

Envision what a life of significance looks like to you. Define the impact you want to make in the world and the areas where you wish to bring about meaningful change.

Evaluate Your Current Situation

Assess your current circumstances, including your career, relationships, and lifestyle. Determine how well they align with your desired pursuit of significance. Identify areas where adjustments may be needed.

Set Goals

Set clear, actionable goals that are aligned with your vision of significance. Break them into smaller, manageable steps you can achieve over time.

Seek Guidance and Mentoring

Connect with individuals who have already transitioned from success to a life of significance. Seek mentors or like-minded communities that can provide support, guidance, and accountability on your journey.

Take Intentional Action

Begin taking deliberate steps toward significance. This may involve changing your career, pursuing opportunities to serve others, or using your influence and resources to make a positive impact. Embrace growth and learning along the way.

Stay Committed

Remaining committed to your pursuit of significance requires perseverance and dedication. Stay focused on your vision, regularly evaluate your progress, course-correct as needed, and continually reaffirm your commitment to living a life of significance.

SECTION 2

STEWARDSHIP

7

Defining and Understanding Stewardship

Beyond a mere abstract notion, stewardship embodies a practical and transformative approach to managing tangible and intangible resources with a deep sense of care and accountability. In this context, stewardship refers to the responsible and ethical management of resources, including money, with a deep awareness of its impact on individuals, communities, and the world.

World Religions on Money

While each religion has unique beliefs and practices, common themes emerge regarding wealth, material possessions, and the spiritual implications of money. The similarities and contrasts among different faith traditions highlight stewardship's importance.

Simplicity and Contentment

Many world religions emphasize simplicity and contentment, advocating detachment from material desires and a focus on inner fulfillment. Buddhism, Hinduism, and Jainism, for example, promote the idea of detachment from material possessions and the cultivation of contentment as a path to spiritual enlightenment. While some religions view simplicity as a virtue to be pursued, others, such as Christianity, Judaism, and Islam, acknowledge the value of wealth but emphasize responsible stewardship and generosity.

Generosity and Compassion

Virtues like generosity, charity, and compassion are celebrated in various religious teachings, underscoring the importance of sharing wealth with others. Christianity, Islam, and Sikhism, among others, emphasize the act of giving, whether through tithing, almsgiving, or charitable acts, as a means to express love for fellow human beings and promote social justice. While some religions encourage giving for the benefit of others, others, such as Buddhism, may emphasize detachment from material wealth to alleviate suffering.

Ethical Earning and Honest Commerce

The ethical acquisition of wealth and fair business practices are emphasized across different religious traditions. For instance, Christianity, Islam, and Hinduism stress the importance of honest labor, fair trade, and integrity in financial transactions. While some religions advocate for modesty and caution against the pursuit of excessive wealth, others view wealth as a blessing from God but emphasize the ethical use of resources for the betterment of society.

Detachment and Transcendence

Several religions teach that attachment to wealth and material possessions can hinder spiritual growth and enlightenment. For example, Buddhism, Jainism, and Taoism emphasize the impermanence of material wealth and the need to cultivate detachment to achieve spiritual liberation. In contrast, religions like Judaism and Christianity acknowledge the value of material blessings and emphasize responsible stewardship, highlighting the transformation of wealth into a force for good.

Personal Responsibility and Accountability

Many religions stress the individual's responsibility to use money and resources wisely and to be accountable for their financial actions. Judaism, Christianity, and Islam, among others, teach the importance of personal responsibility, accountability, and the consequences of one's financial choices in this life and the hereafter. While some religions emphasize personal responsibility for one's economic well-being, others emphasize reliance on a higher power and surrendering financial concerns.

Ceremonial or Symbolic Use of Money

Many religions use money in symbolic or ritualistic ways, such as offering donations or gifts during religious festivals or ceremonies. In some cases, money is viewed as a means of honoring or communicating with the divine.

While each religion has its unique perspectives, shared values and principles underscore the importance of responsible stewardship, generosity, ethical earning, detachment, and personal accountability. By understanding these similarities and contrasts, you gain a broader perspective on the intersection of money and spirituality, inviting you to reflect on your beliefs and practices concerning wealth.

Multifaceted Christian Stewardship

Christian stewardship is the responsible and faithful management of the resources that God has entrusted to you. Time is a precious resource, and as a steward, you are called to use it wisely and intentionally for God's purposes. Your talents and abilities are gifts from God, and you are to use them to serve others and bring glory to Him.

The multifaceted nature of Christian stewardship is based on the biblical foundations of stewardship and the practical implications of being a faithful steward in all areas of your life. While financial stewardship is essential, Christian stewardship goes beyond that to encompass the broader concept of managing all aspects of your resources in a way that honors God.

As you embark on this exploration of Christian stewardship, may your hearts be open to the transforming power of understanding and embracing your role as a faithful caretaker of God's resources. May you adopt a stewardship mindset that permeates every aspect of your life and leads you to use God's gifts wisely for His glory.

God Owns It All

Central to Christian stewardship is the understanding that God owns everything. It is not merely a theological concept but a transformative perspective that shapes your approach to handling the resources entrusted to you. As you grasp the truth that everything you have belongs to God, you begin to view yourself not as an owner but as a steward called to manage His resources wisely and faithfully.

> The earth is the Lord's, and everything in it, the world, and all who live in it (Psalm 24:1, NIV).

> "The silver is Mine, and the gold is Mine," says the Lord of hosts (Haggai 2:8, NKJV).

This foundational belief sets the stage for responsible stewardship, as it reminds you that your role is not to possess and accumulate for yourself but rather to faithfully manage and deploy what has been entrusted to your care.

Being Faithful

Entrusted with the responsibility to manage His resources with wisdom and integrity, your faithfulness in managing small resources reflects your trustworthiness in handling greater duties.

> Moreover it is required in stewards that one be found faithful (1 Corinthians 4:2, NKJV).

> Whoever can be trusted with very little can also be trusted with much, and whoever is dishonest with very little will also be dishonest with much (Luke 16:10, NIV).

The parable in Luke 16 explores the vital connection between faithfulness in small matters and your preparedness for greater responsibilities. It reminds you to approach all aspects of life with integrity and devotion, knowing that God values your faithfulness in every area.

Managing Resources

Christian stewardship extends beyond finances to include other essential aspects of life. It's being mindful of how you manage your time, talents, relationships, what you deem treasures, your body as the temple of the Holy Spirit, and testimony. Each one of these areas presents unique opportunities and challenges for you as a steward and how to approach them in a way that aligns with God's purposes.

Your Time

You are called to use your time wisely, making the most of every opportunity to serve God's purposes.

> So be careful how you live. Don't live like fools, but like those who are wise. Make the most of every opportunity in these evil days (Ephesians 5:15–16, NLT).

> Teach us to number our days, that we may gain a heart of wisdom (Psalm 90:12, NIV).

Your Talents

Your talents are precious gifts from God, and you are encouraged to employ them for the benefit of others, demonstrating good stewardship.

> As each of you has received a gift (a particular spiritual talent, a gracious divine endowment), employ it for one another as [befits] good trustees of God's many-sided grace [faithful stewards of the extremely diverse powers and gifts granted to Christians by unmerited favor] (1 Peter 4:10, AMPC).

Your Treasures

God's kingdom is a hidden treasure more valuable than anything you deem important on earth.

> Honor the Lord with your wealth, with the firstfruits of all your crops; then your barns will be filled to overflowing, and your vats will brim over with new wine (Proverbs 3:9–10, NIV).

Your Body

Recognizing your body as a temple of the Holy Spirit calls for responsible self-care and honoring God with how you use your physical being.

> And so, dear brothers and sisters, I plead with you to give your bodies to God because of all he has done for you. Let them be a living and holy sacrifice—the kind he will find acceptable. This is truly the way to worship him (Romans 12:1, NLT).

Your Testimony

Your testimony and relationships also present opportunities to exhibit good stewardship by living as a light for others and making the most of every interaction.

> Let your light so shine before men, that they may see your good works and glorify your Father in heaven (Matthew 5:16, NKJV).

Be wise in the way you act toward outsiders; make the most of every opportunity (Colossians 4:5, NIV).

Stewardship as Worship

Stewardship is a form of worship. Managing your resources to honor God is a tangible expression of your gratitude, faith, and devotion to the Lord. King David had a heart of worship and stewardship. His prayer beautifully illustrates this concept.

> David praised the Lord in the presence of the whole assembly, saying, "Praise be to you, Lord, the God of our father Israel, from everlasting to everlasting. Yours, Lord, is the greatness and the power and the glory and the majesty and the splendor, for everything in heaven and earth is yours. Yours, Lord, is the kingdom; you are exalted as head over all.

> Wealth and honor come from you; you are the ruler of all things. In your hands are strength and power to exalt and give strength to all. Now, our God, we give you thanks, and praise your glorious name (1 Chronicles 29:10–13, NIV).

Fulfilling God's Purpose

God has a specific purpose and plans for your life; Christian stewardship is crucial in fulfilling that purpose. As a faithful steward, you seek to align yourself with His will, using your time, talents, resources, and influence to accomplish His purpose and bring glory to His name.

Stewardship is not just about managing things well but understanding your role as an instrument in God's hands and living out His purposes for your life. This foundational principle of the Christian faith emphasizes the importance of managing your resources in a way that honors God and furthers His purpose.

For we are His workmanship, created in Christ Jesus for good works, which God prepared beforehand so that we would walk in them (Ephesians 2:10, NASB).

Giving Lifestyle

A Christian steward embraces a lifestyle of sacrificial giving. Generosity flows naturally from a heart transformed by the Gospel. God's abundant love and Jesus's sacrifice motivate you to selfless giving and service.

[Remember] this: he who sows sparingly and grudgingly will also reap sparingly and grudgingly, and he who sows generously [that blessings may come to someone] will also reap generously and with blessings. Let each one [give] as he has made up his own mind and purposed in his heart, not reluctantly or sorrowfully or under compulsion, for God loves (He takes pleasure in, prizes above other things, and is unwilling to abandon or to do without) a cheerful (joyous, "prompt to do it") giver [whose heart is in his giving] (2 Corinthians 9:6–7, AMPC).

Whoever brings blessing will be enriched, and one who waters will himself be watered (Proverbs 11:25, ESV).

Positive Impact

Faithful stewardship enables you to fulfill your God-given assignments with a positive impact. Managing your resources and responsibilities well positions you to live purposefully and be an effective witness for His kingdom.

His master said to him, "Well done, good and faithful slave. You were faithful with a few things, I will put you in charge of many things; enter the joy of your master" (Matthew 25:21, NASB).

For we are God's masterpiece. He has created us anew in Christ Jesus, so we can do the good things he planned for us long ago (Ephesians 2:10, NLT).

Practical Application

The practical application of Christian stewards is an integrated approach to faith and finances. By setting and aligning your financial goals with biblical values, you can live within your means, avoid reckless borrowing, invest wisely, and save for retirement.

Wealth obtained by fraud dwindles, but he who gathers gradually by [honest] labor will increase [his riches] (Proverbs 13:11, AMP).

Sell your possessions and give to the poor. Provide purses for yourselves that will not wear out, a treasure in heaven that will never fail, where no thief comes near and no moth destroys (Luke 12:33, NIV).

Joyful Generosity

Giving is the key to living a joyful and purposeful life. By developing a mindset of abundance rather than a poverty mentality and recognizing that God is your source, you will always find opportunities to bless someone else. Giving joyfully and generously, you experience a profound sense of fulfillment and purpose. Giving aligns with God's heart of love and compassion.

Each of you should give what you have decided in your heart to give, not reluctantly or under compulsion, for God loves a cheerful giver (2 Corinthians 9:7, NIV).

May you embrace the multifaceted nature of Christian stewardship, allowing it to permeate every aspect of your life and guiding you to use God's gifts wisely for His glory.

8

The Old Testament's View on Money

Delving into the teachings on money in the Old Testament, you'll find wisdom from the experiences of biblical characters and guidance in relevant verses. From stories of wealth and prosperity to lessons on stewardship and generosity, the Old Testament's perspective on wealth and stewardship contains wisdom and practical implications for today.

God's Provision and Blessings

The remarkable story of Joseph is a prime example of God blessing and prospering His servants. Joseph's rise from slavery to becoming Pharaoh's trusted advisor showcases God's ability to provide and bless His faithful servants with financial abundance.

> The Lord was with Joseph, and he was a successful man; and he was in the house of his master the Egyptian. And his master saw that the Lord was with him and that the Lord made all he did to prosper in his hand. So Joseph found favor in his sight, and served him. Then he made him overseer of his house, and all that he had he put under his authority. So it was, from the time that he had made him overseer of his house and all that he had, that the Lord blessed the Egyptian's house for Joseph's sake; and

the blessing of the Lord was on all that he had in the house and in the field. Thus he left all that he had in Joseph's] hand, and he did not know what he had except for the bread which he ate (Genesis 39:2–6, NKJV).

You shall remember the Lord your God, for it is he who gives you power to get wealth, that he may confirm his covenant that he swore to your fathers, as it is this day (Deuteronomy 8:18, ESV).

The blessing of the Lord—it makes [truly] rich, and He adds no sorrow with it [neither does toiling increase it] (Proverbs 10:22, AMPC).

Tithing and Offering

Abraham's giving a tenth of his possessions to Melchizedek illustrates the principle of tithing as an act of worship and acknowledging God's provision.

Then Melchizedek king of Salem brought out bread and wine. He was priest of God Most High, and he blessed Abram, saying, "Blessed be Abram by God Most High, Creator of heaven and earth. And praise be to God Most High, who delivered your enemies into your hand." Then Abram gave him a tenth of everything (Genesis 14:18–20, NIV).

One-tenth of the produce of the land, whether grain from the fields or fruit from the trees, belongs to the Lord and must be set apart to him as holy (Leviticus 27:30, NLT).

Wise Financial Management

Joseph's wise management of resources during times of abundance and scarcity demonstrates the importance of planning, saving, and stewardship (Genesis 41–47).

There is precious treasure and oil in the house of the wise [who prepare for the future], but a short-sighted and foolish man swallows it up and wastes it (Proverbs 21:20, AMP).

Whoever loves money never has enough; whoever loves wealth is never satisfied with their income. This too is meaningless (Ecclesiastes 5:10, NIV).

Be sure you know the condition of your flocks, give careful attention to your herds; for riches do not endure forever, and a crown is not secure for all generations (Proverbs 27:23–24, NIV).

Contentment and Avoiding Greed

Achan's greed and disobedience in taking forbidden plunder resulted in severe consequences for the entire nation, highlighting the dangers of covetousness and the importance of contentment.

Israel has sinned, and they have also transgressed My covenant which I commanded them. For they have even taken some of the accursed things, and have both stolen and deceived; and they have also put it among their own stuff. Therefore the children of Israel could not stand before their enemies, but turned their backs before their enemies, because they have become doomed to destruction. Neither will I be with you anymore, unless you destroy the accursed from among you.

Now Joshua said to Achan, "My son, I beg you, give glory to the Lord God of Israel, and make confession to Him, and tell me now what you have done; do not hide it from me" (Joshua 7:11–12; 19, NKJV).

You shall not covet your neighbor's house. You shall not covet your neighbor's wife, or his male or female servant, his ox or donkey, or anything that belongs to your neighbor (Exodus 20:17, NIV).

He who is of a proud heart stirs up strife, but he who trusts in the Lord will be prospered (Proverbs 28:25, NKJV).

Generosity and Care for the Poor

Boaz's compassion and provision for Ruth and Naomi demonstrate the virtue of generosity and caring for the vulnerable, offering a model for how you should treat those in need.

Is it not to share your food with the hungry and to provide the poor wanderer with shelter—when you see the naked, to clothe them, and not to turn away from your own flesh and blood? (Isaiah 58:7, NIV).

He has given freely to the poor, his righteousness endures forever; his horn will be exalted in honor (Psalm 112:9, NASB).

One who is gracious to a poor person lends to the Lord, and He will repay him for his good deed (Proverbs 19:17, NASB).

Trusting God's Provision

Through the miracle of sustained provision, Elijah and the widow of Zarephath experienced God's faithfulness and provision even in times of scarcity.

She went away and did as Elijah had told her. So there was food every day for Elijah and for the woman and her family. For the jar of flour was not used up and the jug of oil did not run dry, in keeping with the word of the Lord spoken by Elijah (1 Kings 17:15–16, NIV).

I have been young, and now am old, yet I have not seen the righteous forsaken or his children begging for bread (Psalm 37:25, ESV).

Keep deception and lies far from me, give me neither poverty nor riches; feed me with the food that is my portion, so that I will not be full and deny You and say, "Who is the Lord?" And that I will not become impoverished and steal, and profane the name of my God (Proverbs 30:8–9, NASB).

Honest and Fair Dealing

The Law required merchants and employers to be honest in their dealings and to pay their workers fairly (Leviticus 19:13; Proverbs 11:1; Jeremiah 22:13).

You shall not oppress your neighbor or rob him. The wages of a hired worker shall not remain with you all night until the morning (Leviticus 19:13, ESV).

And the Lord says, "What sorrow awaits Jehoiakim, who builds his palace with forced labor. He builds injustice into its walls, for he makes his neighbors work for nothing. He does not pay them for their labor (Jeremiah 22:13, NLT).

A false balance and dishonest business practices are extremely offensive to the Lord, but an accurate scale is His delight (Proverbs 11:1, AMP).

Avoiding Debt

The Bible warns against excessive debt and emphasizes the importance of paying back what is owed.

The rich rules over the poor, and the borrower is servant to the lender (Proverbs 22:7, NKVJ).

If you lend money to one of my people among you who is needy, do not treat it like a business deal; charge no interest. If you take your neighbor's cloak as a pledge, return it by sunset, because that cloak is the only covering your neighbor has. What else can they sleep in? When they cry out to me, I will hear, for I am compassionate (Exodus 22:25–27, NIV).

Saving and Planning

Proverbs promote hard work, saving, and planning for the future.

Dishonest money dwindles away, but whoever gathers money little by little makes it grow (Proverbs 13:11, NIV).

The plans of the diligent lead to profit as surely as haste leads to poverty (Proverbs 21:5, NIV).

Take a lesson from the ants, you lazybones. Learn from their ways and become wise! Though they have no prince or governor or ruler to make them work, they labor hard all summer, gathering food for the winter (Proverbs 6:6–8, NLT).

Solomon's Teaching about Money

Renowned for his immense wealth, wisdom, and extravagant lifestyle, Solomon imparts invaluable insights into the principles of money and possessions. Proverbs and Ecclesiastes reflect Solomon's teachings on wealth, stewardship, and the pursuit of true wisdom.

RYAN BOURQUE, CPA, MBT, CKA

Source of True Wealth

Solomon encouraged his readers to seek God's financial guidance and trust in His provision.

> The blessing of the LORD brings wealth, without painful toil for it (Proverbs 10:22, NIV).

> One who trusts in his riches will fall, but the righteous will flourish like the green leaf (Proverbs 11:28, NASB).

> Don't wear yourself out trying to get rich. Be wise enough to know when to quit. In the blink of an eye wealth disappears, for it will sprout wings and fly away like an eagle (Proverbs 23:4–5, NLT).

> Trust in the Lord with all your heart, and do not rely on your own understanding; in all your ways know him, and he will make your paths straight (Proverbs 3:5–6, CSB).

Value of Diligence and Hard Work

Solomon stressed the importance of hard work and diligence, noting that laziness leads to poverty.

> Idle hands make one poor, but diligent hands bring riches (Proverbs 10:4, CSB).

> Work brings profit, but mere talk leads to poverty! (Proverbs 14:23, NLT).

> Do you see a man diligent and skillful in his business? He will stand before kings; he will not stand before obscure men (Proverbs 22:29, AMPC).

Perils of Greed and Materialism

Solomon issues a stern warning against the dangers of greed and materialism.

> He who is greedy for unjust gain troubles his own household, but he who hates bribes will live (Proverbs 15:27, AMPC).

> The greedy stir up conflict, but those who trust in the LORD will prosper (Proverbs 28:25, NIV).

Wisdom in Financial Management

Solomon advocates wise financial management to achieve prosperity.

> The plans of the diligent lead to profit as surely as haste leads to poverty (Proverbs 21:5, NIV).

> A stingy man[a] hastens after wealth and does not know that poverty will come upon him (Proverbs 28:22, ESV).

Blessings of Generosity and Giving

Solomon taught that those who are generous and give to others will receive blessings from God.

> One person gives freely, yet gains even more; another withholds unduly, but comes to poverty. A generous person will prosper; whoever refreshes others will be refreshed (Proverbs 11:24–25, NIV).

> He who has pity on the poor lends to the Lord, and He will pay back what he has given (Proverbs 19:17, NKJV).

Vanity of Material Pursuits

Solomon cautions against the futility of pursuing wealth for its own sake.

> He who loves silver will not be satisfied with silver; nor he who loves abundance, with increase. This also is vanity (Ecclesiastes 5:10, NKJV).

> When all has been heard, the conclusion of the matter is this: fear God and keep his commands, because this is for all humanity (Ecclesiastes 12:13, CSB).

Seeking True Wisdom and Understanding

Solomon emphasized that wisdom and understanding are more valuable than wealth and riches and can help you make sound financial decisions.

> For the Lord gives wisdom; from his mouth come knowledge and understanding (Proverbs 2:6, CSB).

> The reverent and worshipful fear of the Lord is the beginning (the chief and choice part) of Wisdom, and the knowledge of the Holy One is insight and understanding (Proverbs 9:10, AMPC).

> How much better to get wisdom than gold, to get insight rather than silver! (Proverbs 16:16, NIV).

The Old Testament teaches that money and wealth are resources that should be used in ways that honor God and benefit others. Honesty, fairness, and diligence are all essential values related to financial matters. Along with these practical teachings, the Bible emphasizes the importance of trusting in God's provision, living with contentment and gratitude, practicing wise financial management, and cultivating a heart of generosity. By applying these timeless principles to your life, you can navigate the complexities of money with integrity and purpose, honoring God and impacting the lives of others.

9

Jesus on Money Principles

Jesus's teachings on money and possessions hold profound significance, with about one in ten verses in the Gospels addressing stewardship, finances, and possessions. Clearly, these teachings on money, possessions, and the kingdom of God are essential aspects of being a Christian and a kingdom builder.

Through His parables, teachings, and interactions with people, Jesus offers invaluable insights into your relationship with wealth, the dangers of materialism, and the eternal significance of prioritizing the kingdom of God above all else.

Love of Money

Jesus taught that the love of money is the root of all kinds of evil. People like to quote these scriptures thinking money is evil. Money is not bad; God loves to bless His people with spiritual and material blessings. However, it is wrong when money and possessions are more important than your love for God.

> No one can serve two masters. For you will hate one and love the other; you will be devoted to one and despise the other. You cannot serve God and be enslaved to money (Matthew 6:24, NLT).

For the love of money is a root of all kinds of evil. Some people, eager for money, have wandered from the faith and pierced themselves with many griefs (1 Timothy 6:10, NIV).

Kingdom Values and Eternal Treasures

Jesus urges you not to store up treasures on earth, which are vulnerable to decay and theft, but to accumulate eternal treasures in heaven. Do not store up for yourselves treasures on earth, where moths and vermin destroy, and where thieves break in and steal. But store up for yourselves treasures in heaven, where moths and vermin do not destroy, and where thieves do not break in and steal. For where your treasure is, there your heart will be also (Matthew 6:19–21, NIV).

God's Provision and Trust

Jesus taught that material possessions should not be your life's focus, but you should seek the kingdom of God first and trust that God will provide for your needs.

That is why I tell you not to worry about everyday life—whether you have enough food and drink, or enough clothes to wear. Isn't life more than food, and your body more than clothing? Look at the birds. They don't plant or harvest or store food in barns, for your heavenly Father feeds them. And aren't you far more valuable to him than they are? Can all your worries add a single moment to your life? (Matthew 6:25–27, NLT)

So don't worry about these things, saying, "What will we eat? What will we drink? What will we wear?" These things dominate the thoughts of unbelievers, but your heavenly Father already knows all your needs. Seek the Kingdom of

God above all else, and live righteously, and he will give
you everything you need (Matthew 6:31–33, NLT).

Generosity and Sacrificial Giving

Jesus commends the widow who gave all she had, highlighting the value of
sacrificial giving and the heart behind it. He encouraged His followers to
give selflessly without expecting anything in return.

> And Jesus sat down opposite the treasury, and began
> watching how the people were putting money into the
> treasury; and many rich people were putting in large
> amounts. And a poor widow came and put in two lepta
> coins, which amount to a quadrans. Calling His disciples
> to Him, He said to them, "Truly I say to you, this poor
> widow put in more than all the contributors to the
> treasury; for they all put in out of their surplus, but she,
> out of her poverty, put in all she owned, all she had to live
> on" (Mark 12:41–44, NASB).

> Give, and it will be given to you. They will pour into your
> lap a good measure—pressed down, shaken together, and
> running over [with no space left for more]. For with the
> standard of measurement you use [when you do good
> to others], it will be measured to you in return (Luke
> 6:38, AMP).

Contentment and Detachment

Jesus warns against covetousness and emphasizes that life is not about
material abundance.

> And he said to them, "Take care, and be on your guard
> against all covetousness, for one's life does not consist in
> the abundance of his possessions" (Luke 12:15, ESV).

Blessed and fortunate and happy and spiritually prosperous (in that state in which the born-again child of God enjoys His favor and salvation) are those who hunger and thirst for righteousness (uprightness and right standing with God), for they shall be completely satisfied! (Matthew 5:6, AMPC).

Prioritizing People Over Possessions

Jesus urges you to prioritize people over possessions. Acts of kindness reflect God's heart.

Then Jesus said to his host, "When you give a luncheon or dinner, do not invite your friends, your brothers or sisters, your relatives, or your rich neighbors; if you do, they may invite you back and so you will be repaid. But when you give a banquet, invite the poor, the crippled, the lame, the blind, and you will be blessed. Although they cannot repay you, you will be repaid at the resurrection of the righteous" (Luke 14:12–14, NIV).

Giving to the Poor

Jesus taught that those who have should give to those in need and that caring for people in need is equivalent to caring for Jesus Himself.

The King will answer and say to them, "I assure you and most solemnly say to you, to the extent that you did it for one of these brothers of Mine, even the least of them, you did it for Me" (Matthew 25:40, AMP).

Stewardship

Jesus taught that you are a steward of the resources and blessings that God has given you and that you will be held accountable for how you use them.

He who is faithful in what is least is faithful also in much; and he who is unjust in what is least is unjust also in much. Therefore if you have not been faithful in the unrighteous mammon, who will commit to your trust the true riches? And if you have not been faithful in what is another man's, who will give you what is your own? (Luke 16:10–12, NKJV).

Jesus's Parables About Money and Possession

Jesus often used parables to teach important lessons about money and possessions. About sixteen of His parables deal with stewardship, possessions, and finances directly or indirectly.

Parable of the Talents (Matthew 25:14–30; Luke 19:12–17)

A master entrusts his servants with various amounts of money (talents) before going on a journey. Two of the servants invest and double their talents, while the third buries his and returns only what was given to him. The master commends the first two servants for their faithful stewardship but punishes the third for his laziness and lack of investment. This parable illustrates the importance of stewardship, using your resources wisely, and investing them in the kingdom of God.

Parable of the Rich Fool (Luke 12:13–21)

A wealthy man decides to store up all of his surplus grain and goods to build bigger barns and enjoy a leisurely retirement. However, God tells him he will die that night, leaving his riches for someone else to enjoy. Jesus warns against the dangers of greed, materialism, and the foolishness of placing your hope in earthly possessions and pursuing wealth without regard for God's purposes.

Parable of the Good Samaritan (Luke 10:25–37)

The Samaritan, whom the Jewish people despised, takes care of a man who has been robbed, beaten, and left for dead, demonstrating the love and kindness that should characterize your interactions. Although not strictly a parable about money and possessions, Jesus uses this story to illustrate the importance of showing mercy and compassion to those in need, regardless of societal or economic status.

Parable of the Rich Young Ruler (Matthew 19:16–21)

Jesus challenges the young man to sell his possessions and follow Him, highlighting the importance of choosing God over worldly wealth. Although technically not a parable, it conveys a powerful message of aligning your priorities with God's will in stewardship, money, and possessions. The story challenges you to examine your heart, assess the role of wealth in your life, and how willing you are to sacrifice for the sake of God's kingdom.

Parable of the Unforgiving Debtor (Matthew 18:21–35)

While this parable centers on forgiveness, it also highlights the importance of recognizing God's grace and being gracious to others financially. God's forgiveness is immeasurable, and you should reflect that same attitude by showing mercy and generosity toward others, even in financial debts owed to you.

Parable of the Two Debtors (Luke 7:41–43)

This parable teaches about gratitude and recognizing the forgiveness of God, which can affect your approach to stewardship. A moneylender cancels the debts of two debtors who couldn't pay. The forgiven debtor who owed much is more grateful because he realizes the magnitude of his debt being wiped away. Similarly, when you understand the grace and forgiveness God has shown you, you can become a more generous and thankful steward.

Parable of the Faithful and Wise Servant
(Matthew 24:45–51; Luke 12:42–48)

A master entrusted a servant with overseeing his household and providing food to the other servants. The parable highlights the significance of faithful stewardship, diligence, and responsibility in serving God and others, with the understanding that you will be held accountable for handling what God has given you.

Parable of Counting the Cost (Luke 14:28–33)

Jesus uses the analogy of a builder and a king preparing for war to illustrate the importance of counting costs before making significant commitments. Although the parable is about the actual cost of discipleship, it also teaches that stewardship also means considering the long-term implications of your decisions.

Parable of the Prodigal Son (Luke 15:11–32)

The parable demonstrates God's lavish love, grace, and forgiveness toward His children. The younger son's actions represent the tendency to squander the blessings and resources God has given by making poor choices and straying from His ways. Just as the father gave his son an inheritance, God entrusts you with resources, including time, talents, finances, relationships, and opportunities.

Parable of Laborers in the Vineyard (Matthew 20:1–16)

A landowner hired laborers at different times of the day but paid them all the same wage. This parable about the kingdom of God highlights the importance of contentment and not being envious of others' blessings. God's generosity is the same for all, regardless of when you come into His service. You should be content with what God has provided for you and not be jealous of others' possessions or achievements.

Parable of the Rich Man and Lazarus (Luke 16:19–31)

Jesus warns against the dangers of greed and neglecting those in need. The rich man in the story ignores the suffering beggar Lazarus, and both end up in contrasting afterlife situations. It emphasizes the need to be compassionate and generous with our resources, especially toward those less fortunate.

Parable of the Shrewd Manager (Luke 16:1–13)

A dishonest manager is commended for his shrewdness in securing future provisions by reducing the debts owed to his master. Jesus uses this parable to teach about the importance of being wise with money and resources, even though the manager's dishonesty is not condoned. You should use your financial resources to bless others and advance God's kingdom.

Parable of the Friend in Need (Luke 11:5–8)

The man goes to his friend at an inconvenient time to ask for bread to feed his unexpected guest. Despite the initial refusal, the man persists in asking until his friend provides what he needs. This parable teaches the importance of persistence in prayer, seeking God's provision, and approaching stewardship with a humble acknowledgment of your dependence on God. By cultivating a heart of generosity and compassion, you can use your resources to meet the needs of others and glorify God through responsible stewardship.

Parable of Hidden Treasure (Matthew 13:44)

This parable emphasizes the supreme value of the kingdom of God. When a man discovers a hidden treasure, he joyfully sells all he has to possess it. It encourages sacrificial stewardship, demonstrating that investing in the kingdom of God is worth giving up worldly possessions for.

Parable of the Pearl of Great Price (Matthew 13:45–46)

Similar to the previous parable, this one stresses the worth of God's kingdom. A merchant finds a valuable pearl and sells everything to acquire it. It teaches that the kingdom of God should be your highest priority and that you should be willing to give up everything to follow Jesus.

Parable of the Lost Coin (Luke 15:8–9)

Though primarily about the value of each individual soul to God, this parable can also teach about responsible financial stewardship. The woman diligently searches for her lost coin, signifying that you should value what you have been entrusted with and use it wisely for God's purposes.

Jesus taught that money and possessions are not inherently evil but can be dangerous when they become idols or distract you from God. He emphasized the importance of generosity, compassion for the poor, and trust in God's provision.

10

Contentment

Contentment is a virtue beyond mere satisfaction with circumstances; it is a state of inner peace and fulfillment that transcends worldly desires. It is finding true satisfaction in Jesus Christ. Contentment is grounded in your relationship with Christ and the understanding that He is your ultimate source of joy.

Contentment in Biblical Examples

Throughout the Bible, you will find stories and passages that exemplify the virtue of contentment. Job in the Old Testament and the apostle Paul in the New Testament are prime examples of being content irrespective of your circumstances.

The Apostle Paul

Despite facing numerous trials and challenges, the apostle Paul displayed contentment in all circumstances.

> Not that I speak from [any personal] need, for I have learned to be content [and self-sufficient through Christ, satisfied to the point where I am not disturbed or uneasy]

regardless of my circumstances. I know how to get along and live humbly [in difficult times], and I also know how to enjoy abundance and live in prosperity. In any and every circumstance I have learned the secret [of facing life], whether well-fed or going hungry, whether having an abundance or being in need (Philippians 4:11–12, AMP).

Job

Job, a man of great righteousness, experienced profound suffering and loss. Yet, amidst his trials, he maintained his trust in God and found contentment in His sovereignty. Job 1:21 reflects his perspective.

> He said, "Naked I came from my mother's womb, and naked I shall return there. The Lord gave and the Lord has taken away. Blessed be the name of the Lord," (Job 1:21, NASB).

Relationship with Christ

Finding contentment in your relationship with God is crucial. True contentment comes from knowing and trusting Christ rather than external circumstances.

> Whom have I in heaven but you? And earth has nothing I desire besides you (Psalm 73:25, NIV).

Seeking God's Will

You experience contentment when you align your desires with God's will. True satisfaction is found when you seek to live according to God's plan.

> Fear of the Lord leads to life, bringing security and protection from harm (Proverbs 19:23, NLT).

Foundation for Financial Freedom

Contentment is a foundation for wise financial decisions. Material possessions do not measure true financial success but by aligning your finances with God's priorities. True contentment comes from a deep gratitude for what you have rather than a longing for what you don't have and always wanting more or what others have.

> Do not store up for yourselves treasures on earth, where moths and vermin destroy, and where thieves break in and steal. But store up for yourselves treasures in heaven, where moths and vermin do not destroy, and where thieves do not break in and steal. For where your treasure is, there your heart will be also (Matthew 6:19– 21, NIV).

Contentment in God Alone

Contentment comes from finding satisfaction in God alone. By recognizing that He is your portion and inheritance that surpasses any world possession, you can be content in any circumstance. Combining godliness with contentment is a valuable treasure reflecting a heart that prioritizes God above all else.

> The Lord is my chosen portion and my cup; you hold my lot. The lines have fallen for me in pleasant places; indeed, I have a beautiful inheritance (Psalm 16:5–6, ESV).

> But godliness with contentment is great gain (1 Timothy 6:6, CSB).

> Whom have I in heaven but you? And there is nothing on earth that I desire besides you. My flesh and my heart may fail, but God is the strength of my heart and my portion forever (Psalm 73:25–26, ESV).

KINGDOM BUILDERS PLAYBOOK

Peaceful Heart vs. Envy

While contentment brings peace to your heart and positively impacts your well-being, envy leads to dissatisfaction and emotional turmoil. If you are content with God's presence within you, you will live a life where the fruit of the Spirit flows and flourishes within you, promoting love, joy, and peace.

> A heart at peace gives life to the body, but envy rots the bones (Proverbs 14:30, NIV).

> But the fruit of the Spirit is love, joy, peace, patience, kindness, goodness, faithfulness, gentleness, self-control; against such things, there is no law (Galatians 5:22–23, NASB).

True Happiness

Pursuing wealth and possessions can never fully satisfy nor bring happiness. Contentment comes from seeking God and trusting in His provision. Contentment is found in trusting God's care and not being preoccupied with material needs.

> Those who love money will never have enough. How meaningless to think that wealth brings true happiness! (Ecclesiastes 5:10, NLT).

Opposing Greed and Materialism

Contentment opposes the lure of greed and materialism, recognizing that true life is not defined by abundant possessions. Instead, it focuses on aligning your mind with God's will, not conforming to the world's desires for material possessions but valuing eternal over earthy things.

> Then He said to them, "Watch out and guard yourselves against every form of greed; for not even when one has

an overflowing abundance does his life consist of nor is it derived from his possessions," (Luke 12:15, AMP).

Do not be conformed to this world, but be transformed by the renewal of your mind, that by testing you may discern what is the will of God, what is good and acceptable and perfect (Romans 12:2, ESV).

Trusting in God Always

Contentment is learned by always trusting God in abundance or lack. Steadfast trust in God leads to inner peace and contentment.

> You will keep in perfect peace all who trust in you, all whose thoughts are fixed on you! (Isaiah 26:3, NLT).

> Lord, my heart is not proud; my eyes are not haughty. I do not get involved with things too great or too wondrous for me. Instead, I have calmed and quieted my soul like a weaned child with its mother; my soul is like a weaned child (Psalm 131:1–2, CSB).

Combining godliness with contentment is a valuable treasure reflecting a heart that prioritizes God above all else.

> But godliness with contentment is great gain (1 Timothy 6:6, CSB).

Assurance and Security

When you recognize God's faithful presence and provision, contentment brings assurance and security. Contentment arises from knowing that He will never fail you, give up on you, or leave you without support. Within this assurance and security, you can cast your worries and anxieties on Him and find rest in His care.

Contentment is rooted in gratitude and embracing God's plan for your life. Resist the temptation of comparing yourself to others and instead focus on fulfilling your unique purpose.

Let your character or moral disposition be free from love of money [including greed, avarice, lust, and craving for earthly possessions] and be satisfied with your present [circumstances and with what you have]; for He [God] Himself has said, I will not in any way fail you nor give you up nor leave you without support. [I will] not, [I will] not, [I will] not in any degree leave you helpless nor forsake nor let [you] down (relax My hold on you) [Assuredly not!] (Hebrews 13:5, AMPC).

Casting all your cares [all your anxieties, all your worries, and all your concerns, once and for all] on Him, for He cares about you [with deepest affection, and watches over you very carefully] (1 Peter 5:7, AMP).

Acknowledging That God Provides

Contentment stems from recognizing that God's provision meets your basic needs. Contentment arises from acknowledging that all good things come from God, the unchanging source of blessings. Finding delight in God, making Him the ultimate Source of your joy and fulfillment.

If we have food and clothing, we will be content with these (1 Timothy 6:8, CSB).

Every good gift and every perfect gift is from above, coming down from the Father of lights, with whom there is no variation or shadow due to change (James 1:17, ESV).

Delight yourself also in the Lord, and He will give you the desires and secret petitions of your heart (Psalm 37:4, AMPC).

Prayer Lifestyle

You experience contentment through prayerful surrender to God and receiving His peace that surpasses all human understanding. Cultivate contentment by fixing your thoughts on eternal values and heavenly perspectives.

> Do not be anxious about anything, but in everything by prayer and pleading with thanksgiving let your requests be made known to God. And the peace of God, which surpasses all comprehension, will guard your hearts and minds in Christ Jesus (Philippians 4:6–7, NASB).

Cultivate contentment by fixing your thoughts on eternal values and heavenly perspectives.

> Set your minds on things above, not on earthly things (Colossians 3:2, NIV).

Rest in Jesus

Contentment is discovering rest in Jesus when you surrender your burdens to Him. You are content in knowing that, when you are weak, you can rely on God's grace and power.

> Come to Me, all you who labor and are heavy laden, and I will give you rest. Take My yoke upon you and learn from Me, for I am gentle and lowly in heart, and you will find rest for your souls. For My yoke is easy and My burden is light (Matthew 11:28–30, NKJV).

> Each time he said, "My grace is all you need. My power works best in weakness." So now I am glad to boast about my weaknesses, so that the power of Christ can work through me (2 Corinthians 12:9, NLT).

Anchored in God

Hope anchored in God's provision rather than in uncertain wealth fosters contentment. Contentment is recognizing that worldly gain cannot compare to the value of your eternal soul.

> As for the rich in this present world, instruct them not to be conceited and arrogant, nor to set their hope on the uncertainty of riches, but on God, who richly and ceaselessly provides us with everything for our enjoyment (1 Timothy 6:17, AMP).

> For what will it benefit someone if he gains the whole world yet loses his life? Or what will anyone give in exchange for his life? (Matthew 16:26, CSB).

God's Strength and Guidance

Contentment comes through trusting God's guidance and not relying solely on human understanding. Prioritizing God's kingdom above all else and seeking His righteousness are foundational to living a contented life.

> Trust in the Lord with all your heart and do not lean on your own understanding. In all your ways acknowledge Him, and He will make your paths straight (Proverbs 3:5–6, NASB).

> But seek his kingdom, and these things will be given to you as well (Luke 12:31, NIV).

> Lord, my heart is not proud; my eyes are not haughty. I do not get involved with things too great or too wondrous for me. Instead, I have calmed and quieted my soul like a weaned child with its mother; my soul is like a weaned child (Psalm 131:1–2, CSB).

Jesus's Faithfulness

Contentment is grounded in the faithful, unchanging nature of Jesus Christ. He remains constant, and you find contentment in His love and care for you.

> Jesus Christ is the same yesterday and today and forever (Hebrews 13:8, NIV).

God's Goodness

You are content believing God works all things for your good according to His purpose.

> And we know that God causes everything to work together for the good of those who love God and are called according to his purpose for them (Romans 8:28, NLT).

Resist Worldly Desires

Contentment is nurtured when you resist the allure of worldly desires and love God more than the world. Content flows from the assurance that God supplies all your needs according to His abundant riches instead of placing hope in uncertain wealth.

> Do not love the world or the things in the world. If anyone loves the world, the love of the Father is not in him. For all that is in the world—the lust of the flesh, the lust of the eyes, and the pride of life—is not of the Father but is of the world (1 John 2:15–16, NKJV).

Content flows from the assurance that God supplies all your needs according to His abundant riches.

> And this same God who takes care of me will supply all
> your needs from his glorious riches, which have been given
> to us in Christ Jesus (Philippians 4:19, NLT).

These Bible verses emphasize that true contentment is found in seeking God, trusting in His provision, and prioritizing eternal values over worldly desires. Happiness arises from recognizing God's faithfulness, finding peace in His presence, and experiencing His transforming power in your life.

11

Budgeting

Christian budgeting is aligning your financial decisions with biblical principles and stewarding your resources to honor God. Budgeting empowers you to manage your finances wisely as a responsible steward.

Establish a Financial Plan

Budgeting involves estimating and planning expenses before pursuing financial goals and responsibilities. You can set your financial priorities and track expenses by developing a comprehensive financial plan that aligns with your goals, values, and God's Word.

> For which of you, wanting to build a tower, doesn't first sit down and calculate the cost to see if he has enough to complete it? (Luke 14:28, CSB).

Live within Your Means

Budgeting helps you avoid excessive debt that leads to financial hardship and enables you to practice living within your means. You can intentionally spend less than you earn, allowing room for saving and giving.

The rich rule over the poor, and the borrower is the slave to the lender (Proverbs 22:7, ESV).

Give Generously

Cultivate a heart of generosity by faithfully giving back to God and supporting others in need. Budgeting with a spirit of giving and generosity can lead to greater blessing and prosperity, both financially and emotionally.

One person gives freely, yet gains more; another withholds what is right, only to become poor. A generous person will be enriched, and the one who gives a drink of water will receive water (Proverbs 11:24–25, CSB).

He who has pity on the poor lends to the Lord, and He will pay back what he has given (Proverbs 19:17, NKJV).

Save for the Future

Set aside a portion of your income for savings and emergencies. Create an emergency fund and establish long-term savings goals, such as retirement planning and education funds. Budgeting includes financial planning for future generations. Leaving a legacy for descendants through wise financial decisions is considered virtuous.

A good person leaves an inheritance for their children's children, but a sinner's wealth is stored up for the righteous (Proverbs 13:22, NIV).

Seek Wise Counsel

Budgeting with prayerful commitment involves seeking God's guidance in financial matters. When entrusting your plans and budgeting to God, He supports and directs you on managing your finances wisely.

> Commit your work to the Lord, and your plans will be established (Proverbs 16:3, ESV).

Consult trusted advisors or financial professionals who share your Christian values. Seek guidance and wisdom in making financial decisions, especially for significant investments or complex matters.

> Without consultation and wise advice, plans are frustrated, but with many counselors they are established and succeed (Proverbs 15:22, AMP).

Practice Contentment

Find contentment in God and His provision rather than constantly striving for more. Be grateful for what you have and resist the temptation of materialism and consumerism. Budgeting encourages contentment and wise financial management. Pursuing material possessions without contentment can lead to a never-ending cycle of dissatisfaction and debt.

> He who loves money will not be satisfied with money, nor he who loves abundance with its gain. This too is vanity (emptiness) (Ecclesiastes 5:10, AMP).

Avoid Impulsive Purchases

Exercising self-control and discernment when making purchases is crucial for responsible financial management. Avoiding impulsive buying and carefully considering whether a purchase aligns with your values and financial goals can lead to more mindful spending. Careful planning and diligence are essential when managing finances as making wise budgeting choices can lead to economic prosperity, whereas rushing into financial decisions without proper consideration leads to financial difficulties.

> The plans of the diligent lead surely to abundance and advantage, but everyone who acts in haste comes surely to poverty (Proverbs 21:5, AMP).

Your spending habits reflect your priorities and values. Budgeting helps you align your financial decisions with biblical principles instead of being solely driven by worldly desires.

Communicate and Collaborate

If married or in a family setting, openly communicate about finances and work together as a team. Collaborate on budgeting decisions, set shared financial goals, and support each other in stewarding resources.

> Two are better than one because they have a good return for their labor (Ecclesiastes 4:9, NIV).

Regularly Review and Adjust

Regularly review your budget and financial plan to track progress, identify areas of improvement, and make necessary adjustments. Flexibility is crucial in adapting to changing circumstances. Budgeting makes you aware of the state of your resources and assets. Wealth is not guaranteed to last forever, so prudent financial management is essential.

> Be diligent to know the state of your flocks, and look well to your herds; for riches are not forever; does a crown endure to all generations? (Proverbs 27:23–24, AMPC).

Prudence and foresight are crucial in budgeting, proactively identifying potential financial risks, and protecting yourself from financial harm.

> A prudent person sees evil and hides himself; but the naive proceed, and pay the penalty (Proverbs 27:12, NASB).

Seek Financial Freedom

Strive for financial freedom by diligently working toward eliminating debt and managing financial obligations' responsibilities with prudence.

The goal is to live a debt-free life where possible, honoring God with your finances and freeing yourself to serve Him wholeheartedly. Responsible budgeting includes wise borrowing and fulfilling financial commitments, avoiding excessive debt and irresponsible economic behavior.

> The wicked borrow and never repay, but the godly are generous givers (Psalm 37:21, NLT).

Responsible and Ethical Practices

Responsible budgeting with small amounts of money shows trustworthiness, preparing you for more significant financial responsibilities.

> He who is faithful in a very little thing is also faithful in much; and he who is dishonest in a very little thing is also dishonest in much. Therefore if you have not been faithful in the use of earthly wealth, who will entrust the true riches to you? (Luke 16:10–11, AMP).

Budgeting promotes honest and ethical financial practices. Accumulating wealth gradually through hard work and integrity is more sustainable and secure than seeking fast but dishonest gains.

> Wealth from get-rich-quick schemes quickly disappears; wealth from hard work grows over time (Proverbs 13:11, NLT).

Have a Savings Plan

Budgeting emphasizes the wisdom of saving and preparing for unforeseen circumstances, just as the ants gather food during abundant times to sustain themselves during scarcity.

> Go to the ant, you sluggard; consider its ways and be wise! It has no commander, no overseer or ruler, yet it stores

its provisions in summer and gathers its food at harvest (Proverbs 6:6–8, NIV).

Be Grateful

Budgeting helps manage wealth and resources, reflecting gratitude to God and a willingness to share with others. Focusing on generosity and using your wealth to help others build a meaningful life beyond material possessions.

> As for the rich in this world, charge them not to be proud and arrogant and contemptuous of others, nor to set their hopes on uncertain riches, but on God, Who richly and ceaselessly provides us with everything for [our] enjoyment. [Charge them] to do good, to be rich in good works, to be liberal and generous of heart, ready to share [with others], in this way laying up for themselves [the riches that endure forever as] a good foundation for the future, so that they may grasp that which is life indeed (1 Timothy 6:17–19, AMPC).

Prioritize God First

When budgeting, you should prioritize spiritual values over money and material possessions. Your devotion should be to serving God and others rather than only being driven by financial gain. Approach your budgeting and financial decisions with a spirit of gratitude and generosity, recognizing that you are merely stewards of what He has entrusted to you.

> But who am I, and who are my people, that we should be able to offer so willingly as this? For all things come from You, and of Your own we have given You (1 Chronicles 29:14, NKJV).

Reflect on the consequences of neglecting to prioritize God in your financial life. When you focus solely on financial gain without considering

God's principles, you may find that your efforts yield little satisfaction and fulfillment. Instead, put God first in your budgeting and financial planning, and He will bless your endeavors and fill your life with purpose and abundance.

> Now then, the Lord of armies says this: "Consider your ways! You have sown much, only to harvest little; you eat, but there is not enough to be satisfied; you drink, but there is not enough to become drunk; you put on clothing, but there is not enough for anyone to get warm; and the one who earns, earns wages to put into a money bag full of holes" (Haggai 1:5–6, NASB).

Principles on Creating Your Budget

Creating and managing a budget is fundamental to achieving financial goals. By budgeting, you can make informed decisions and work toward long-term goals. These essential principles will help you navigate your budgeting process effectively.

Create a Written Budget

Create a written budget for allocating income, tracking expenses, and setting financial goals. A written budget provides an organized overview of your financial situation for making informed financial decisions regarding fund allocation, setting and tracking goals, awareness of spending habits, and accountability for attaining financial freedom and building wealth.

Simple and Straightforward

Keep your budgeting approach simple and easy to understand. Avoid overcomplicating things with elaborate spreadsheets or complicated software. Instead, opt for a straightforward method that works best for you, like a basic spreadsheet or pen and paper. Simplicity encourages consistency and makes budgeting more manageable in the long run.

Start with Your Income

Your budget should always begin with your income. Calculate your total monthly income after deducting taxes and other essential deductions. Knowing how much you have available that you can spend is the foundation for smart financial planning.

Prioritize Based on Values and Goals

Budgeting is not merely about tracking expenses, but it's about aligning your spending with your values and long-term objectives. Take the time to reflect on your priorities and identify what truly matters to you. Allocate funds accordingly, ensuring that your budget reflects what you value most in life.

Track Your Income and Expenses

Before creating a budget, you need to know how much money is coming in and going out each month. Use an app or a spreadsheet to track your income and expenses for at least a month. This will give you an estimate of what you actually spend to what you think.

Categorize Your Expenses

Categorize your expenses to gain a clear understanding of where your money goes. Separate fixed expenses, like rent, mortgage payments, and utilities, from variable costs, such as dining out or entertainment. This categorization will help you analyze your spending patterns and make informed adjustments.

Set a Savings Goal

Saving should be a cornerstone of your budget. Determine a specific savings goal, such as saving a certain percentage of your income each month. Prioritize saving for emergencies, future plans, and retirement. Automate your savings process to ensure regular contributions, even if it's a small amount initially.

Apportion Your Income

You can have a unique budget tailored to your financial needs, goals, and planning by apportioning your income. Start with honoring God with your tithes and offerings. Then allocate money to the other categories by starting from the essentials like food and housing to the wants and the luxuries last.

Live Within Your Means

Avoid falling into the trap of spending beyond your means. Live below your income and prioritize needs over wants. Steer clear of unnecessary debt and be cautious with credit cards. Spending less than you earn builds a solid financial foundation and reduces stress.

Review and Adjust Regularly

Life is dynamic and circumstances change. Regularly review your budget and adjust it as needed to accommodate new priorities, changes in income, or unexpected expenses. Flexibility in your budgeting approach ensures it remains relevant and effective over time.

Creating a budget, trusting in God's provision, and being a good steward ensure financial planning and decision-making that are tailored to your needs and goals. By tracking your income and expenses, categorizing your spending, and prioritizing your goals, you can manage your finances according to biblical principles, achieving financial peace and freedom.

12

Use of Debt

Debt is a prevalent financial tool in today's society, but it is important for Christians to approach it with wisdom and discernment. By aligning your financial decisions with biblical principles and incorporating wisdom from the Bible, you can make informed choices regarding debt.

Here in the United States, people are addicted to debt. Most people make financial decisions based on what the payment is each month versus what something actually costs. I understand that most people are not CPAs and don't have a background like I do in business, which necessitates understanding the numbers.

However, the Bible has a lot to say about debt. The Bible goes so far as to say that the borrower is the slave to the lender.

> The rich rules over the poor, and the borrower is the slave of the lender (Proverbs 22:7, NIV).

Debt History in the US

You have to take debt in a historical context. Though the idea is unheard of in America today and the 13th Amendment of the United States Constitution made it illegal, indentured servitude was a type of barter system in the

1600s. Almost a fifth of the early settlers were indentured servants who agreed to work in exchange for the price of passage to America. Based on the English system, debtors' prisons existed to punish those who couldn't pay their debt. In some cases, people were forced to give up sons and daughters in satisfaction of those debt payments. Today, you can still be sent to jail for fraudulent money matters, but not because you can't pay your debt.

> Owe no one anything except to love one another, for he who loves another has fulfilled the law (Romans 13:8, NKJV).

Can you imagine not only losing your assets but losing your children to a life of slavery? In my opinion, I don't see any valued argument for slavery or that slavery is good. We fought the Civil War on the issue, and societies justified the practice by calling themselves Christians. Clearly, not paying your debts is bad, and the Bible goes as far as to say that someone who doesn't pay their debts is wicked.

> The wicked borrow and never repay, but the godly are generous givers (Psalm 37:21, NLT).

Popular Christian money experts advocate for a debt-free lifestyle. Though I appreciate that sentiment, it isn't practical for many Americans. Making a call for people to live in lower-cost areas to avoid debt also places them in situations where there may be fewer jobs or fewer opportunities for their children for the sake of saving money.

Due to the reliance on and addiction to debt in the US, many homes are underwritten with thirty-year mortgages. I always find it astonishing that someone in America who is eighty-five can get a thirty-year mortgage. The availability of credit and the ease of access to debt have created a dramatic price increase in housing in America. I hate to focus on housing, but for most people you talk to, that is the American dream—the dream to have a stable and consistent place to raise a family and build community.

Fortunately in America, since the 2008 financial crisis was primarily fueled by toxic home loans, underwriters have become stringent in their criteria for lending and work to ensure that people aren't biting off more than they can chew.

I share this background because we have to accept the fact that we live in a society that relies on debt to function. Getting to the point before I digress, I don't like debt, but debt is a necessary tool that is used on a personal level to purchase a home that has tremendous benefits to skilled laborers and manufacturers and promotes building communities and families.

Debt is just about a necessity, especially in the real estate space. Though it would be great to buy an apartment complex with cash, most people cannot, and saving to build a real estate portfolio would take more years to build than you have years on this earth.

Stewardship in the Use of Debt

So my argument is that you can be a good steward and still use debt. You have to make calculated decisions on how you will use debt. Though you can't plan for everything and what will go wrong or the cycles of markets, the responsible use of debt can build wealth and generate resources for kingdom building. Fortunately, our system in the United States encourages calculated risk-taking as there is no debtor prison. Though I don't believe in using the option unless you absolutely have no other choice, you can still get a fresh start and declare bankruptcy.

I advocate for the use of debt in circumstances where it makes sense. Building roads and schools with bonds, parks and community pools, homes, corporate projects, and buyouts, pooling resources and borrowing for the great collective good. I do not advocate borrowing too much for education in many circumstances. I don't advocate borrowing for a car loan if you can save and avoid it and pay cash. I surely do not advocate borrowing from credit cards to spend more money to buy things to impress people you don't even like.

Studies have shown (need to find this study) that people are willing to pay 30 percent more on a credit card for a purchase than if they were paying cash or using their debit card or a check. An MIT study (https://link. springer.com/article/10.1023/A:1008196717017) published in 2001 found that shoppers will spend 100 percent more using their credit cards instead of cash.

Another study found that buying with credit cards activates the reward center of your brain, motivating you to spend more. A massive industry is built around points and perks to get you to spend money on your credit cards. To be important in this society, you need to maximize points.

I am sorry but I don't have one wealthy, successful client who has given credit to their successes in life because of their extensive use of personal credit cards. The interest rates are generally horrific, and if you are lured into a zero-interest rate card or balance transfer by chance, the statistics and probabilities are not on your side. Most people will end up paying interest.

There really is no free money.

Credit card companies cannot run their companies and pay salaries and bonuses off extended free credit. Like the cost of homes in the US, the use of debt has also created an environment where higher education is too expensive and not attainable for most.

Easy money and government-backed loans have created and still make a generation of college graduates with degrees that will likely not give the graduate enough income to pay the debts and require refinancing the debt and loan modification of payment terms. I have a big argument for the value of trade education and guiding students into majors that will help them have meaningful and lucrative careers in something they are good and passionate about. If you are passionate about it, I hope that you use your influence and ability to make a change by addressing some of these fundamental issues.

Sadly, becoming a medical doctor in this country generally takes student loan debt. Seemingly endless schooling and endless hours lead your brightest minds in medicine into mountains of student loan debt that cripple their personal finances for many years to come. The same goes for dentists, and advanced degrees in engineering, law, etc.

So while I'm not too fond of the use of debt in education if you can make a sound financial case for the use of it, meaning that you will be working toward a high-paying job that will have the income to pay it back, then so be it. Taking out $200k in student loan debt for a liberal arts degree with no tie to actually making a good income to pay it back isn't a good use of resources.

Debt seems arguably unavoidable for the youth in America, and though you may use it, do so sparingly and in a calculated manner. It is your duty as a kingdom builder to pay your debts anytime you borrow. In fact, the Lord commands it.

Pay to all what is owed to them: taxes to whom taxes are owed, revenue to whom revenue is owed, respect to whom respect is owed, honor to whom honor is owed (Romans 13:7, NIV).

Use of Debt Best Practices

Minimize Debt

Strive to minimize debt and live within your means. Avoid unnecessary borrowing and carefully consider the long-term implications of taking on debt.

> My son, if you have put up security for your neighbor or entered into an agreement with a stranger, you have been snared by the words of your mouth—trapped by the words from your mouth. Do this, then, my son, and free yourself, for you have put yourself in your neighbor's power: Go, humble yourself, and plead with your neighbor. Don't give sleep to your eyes or slumber to your eyelids. Escape like a gazelle from a hunter, like a bird from a hunter's trap (Proverbs 6:1–5, CSB).

Understand the Risks

Recognize that debt carries risks and obligations. Assess your ability to repay before committing to any financial obligations.

Do not be among those who give pledges [involving themselves in others' finances], or among those who become guarantors for others' debts. If you have nothing with which to pay [another's debt when he defaults], why should his creditor take your bed from under you? (Proverbs 22:26–27, AMP).

Seek Wise Counsel

Seek counsel from trusted financial advisors, mentors, or experts who can provide guidance based on biblical principles and your specific financial situation.

Budget and Save

Develop a budget that prioritizes saving and allows you to build an emergency fund. By saving, you can reduce the need for debt when unexpected expenses arise.

Good planning and hard work lead to prosperity, but hasty shortcuts lead to poverty (Proverbs 21:5, NLT).

Evaluate the Purpose

Evaluate the purpose of the debt. Consider whether it aligns with biblical values and whether the intended use will bring glory to God.

One who lacks sense gives a pledge and puts up security in the presence of his neighbor (Proverbs 17:18, NIV).

Pray for Guidance

Seek God's guidance through prayer and ask for wisdom in financial decision-making. Trust in His provision and seek His direction in matters of debt.

Prioritize Repayment

Commit to honoring your financial obligations and prioritizing debt repayment. Develop a repayment plan that aligns with your financial goals.

> Do not withhold good from those to whom it is due, when it is in your power to do it. Do not say to your neighbor, "Go, and come back, and tomorrow I will give it to you," when you have it with you (Proverbs 3:27–28, NASB).

Practice Contentment

Cultivate a heart of contentment, finding joy and satisfaction in God's provision rather than constantly striving for material possessions.

Learn Financial Literacy

Invest time in improving your financial literacy. Educate yourself about personal finance, budgeting, and wise money management to make informed decisions.

Stay Accountable

Surround yourself with a community of believers who can provide accountability and support in making wise financial choices.

> Let your Yes be simply Yes, and your No be simply No; anything more than that comes from the evil one (Matthew 5:37, AMPC).

Debt use should be cautiously approached and guided by biblical principles. By drawing wisdom from the Bible, you can make sound financial decisions regarding debt. Strive for financial freedom, minimize debt, and honor God with your financial stewardship.

Saddleback Church's financial freedom workshop is designed to help individuals and families get out of debt and gain financial freedom. The workshop is based on the concept of David Ramsey's The Debt Snowball, which was popularized by Dave Ramsey and is also used in his Financial Peace University course. The Debt Snowball strategy involves paying off debts from smallest to largest, starting with the smallest debt and then using the money that would have been paid toward that debt to pay off the next smallest debt and so on, until all debts are paid off.

13

Investing

In the parable of the talents, the two servants who invested the talents were deemed faithful and received more (Matthew 25). Biblical-based investing helps you plan for the future and grow your wealth in God's way, for all your resources belong to God.

Prayer for Discernment

As a kingdom builder, you are a steward of God-given resources and must honor God with your investment choices. Therefore, pray for guidance and discernment when making investment decisions.

> Trust in the Lord with all your heart; do not depend on your own understanding. Seek his will in all you do, and he will show you which path to take (Proverbs 3:5–6, NLT).

Set Clear Financial Goals

Define your investment objectives and time horizon. Determine if you are investing for short-term needs (e.g., emergency fund), medium-term goals (e.g., buying a home), or long-term objectives (e.g., retirement). Having clear goals will help shape your investment strategy.

Invest Debt-Free

Get out of debt first before you start investing money. Investing has risks; you can't afford to lose money when you have debt obligations. Avoid investing with borrowed money.

Diversification

Spread your investments across different asset classes and avoid being tempted into putting all your resources into a single venture. Diversification can help reduce risk, minimizing the impact of a downturn in any particular sector.

> Invest in seven ventures, yes, in eight; you do not know what disaster may come upon the land (Ecclesiastes 11:2, NIV).

Avoid Day Trading and Market Timing

Avoid trying to time the market or make short-term trades; you can lose money on fees, taxes, and commissions. Trying to predict short-term market movements is challenging and often futile. Instead, focus on your long-term investment strategy and avoid making emotional decisions based on the market's ups and downs.

> There is a time for everything, and a season for every activity under the heavens (Ecclesiastes 3:1, NIV).

Ethical Investing

Consider investing in companies or ventures that align with Christian values and principles. Avoid unethical industries or businesses engaged in activities that contradict Christian teachings, such as those related to abortion, pornography, gambling, or harmful products.

Finally brothers and sisters, whatever is true, whatever is honorable, whatever is just, whatever is pure, whatever is lovely, whatever is commendable—if there is any moral excellence and if there is anything praiseworthy—dwell on these things (Philippians 4:8, CSB).

Avoiding Exploitation

Avoid investments that exploit others or contribute to human suffering, such as companies involved in slave labor, unfair wages, or environmental degradation.

Whoever oppresses the poor shows contempt for their Maker, but whoever is kind to the needy honors God (Proverbs 14:31, NIV).

Transparency and Honesty

Seek investments that prioritize transparency and honesty in their business practices. Avoid companies that engage in deceptive or unethical behaviors.

A false balance and unrighteous dealings are extremely offensive and shamefully sinful to the Lord, but a just weight is His delight (Proverbs 11:1, AMPC).

Consistency

Regularly contribute to your investments even if it's a small amount. Consistency in contributing over time can lead to significant growth through the power of compounding.

A faithful person will abound with blessings, but one who hurries to be rich will not go unpunished (Proverbs 28:20, NASB).

Avoid Emotional Investing

Emotional investing, driven by fear or greed, can lead to poor decision-making. Stick to your well-thought-out investment plan even during turbulent times. Guard against the temptation of materialism with successful investing.

> A man's heart plans his way, but the Lord directs his steps (Proverbs 16:9, NKJV).

Risk Tolerance

Understand and assess your risk tolerance. Some investments carry higher risks but also offer the potential for higher returns. Be honest about how much risk you can comfortably handle without losing sleep over market fluctuations.

> The naive or inexperienced person [is easily misled and] believes every word he hears, but the prudent man [is discreet and astute and] considers well where he is going (Proverbs 14:15, AMP).

Long-Term Investing

Investing is typically a long-term endeavor. Time in the market allows your investments to potentially grow and recover from short-term market volatility. Avoid making knee-jerk reactions based on short-term fluctuations.

> Good planning and hard work lead to prosperity, but hasty shortcuts lead to poverty (Proverbs 21:5, NLT).

Investing involves risks with no guarantee of returns. If you're unsure about specific investments or financial decisions, consider seeking guidance from a financial advisor with an understanding of financial matters and Christian values.

Biblically Based Investing and ESG Related to Kingdom Investing

Biblically based investing and ESG (environmental, social, and governance) are complementary approaches to investing. On the one hand, biblically based investing aims to align investments with your Christian beliefs and values by avoiding companies or industries that go against biblical principles. On the other hand, ESG investing seeks to consider the financial returns and the impact of investments on the environment, society, and corporate governance.

Ethical Screening

Biblically based investing involves screening companies and industries according to Christian principles, such as avoiding companies producing or distributing alcohol, tobacco, gambling, or pornography and companies that promote abortion or violate human rights. The investment strategy also promotes companies that operate ethically and socially responsibly.

ESG investing evaluates companies based on environmental impact, social responsibility, and corporate governance practices. ESG investors typically seek out companies that promote sustainability, social justice, and transparency and avoid companies that engage in unethical practices, such as pollution or labor exploitation.

Positive Impact

Both approaches aim to create a positive impact through investment choices. Biblically based investing seeks to support businesses that contribute positively to society and avoid those that may harm it. ESG investing, too, seeks to invest in companies that adhere to sustainable and responsible practices, supporting long-term social and environmental well-being.

Corporate Responsibility

Biblically based investing and ESG investing encourage companies to act responsibly and ethically. Companies that align with these principles are more likely to be transparent, accountable, and committed to corporate social responsibility. This alignment can lead to better corporate governance, reduced reputational risks, and improved long-term financial performance.

Long-Term Perspective

Both approaches often adopt a long-term investment perspective. Investors in these strategies recognize that companies demonstrating ethical solid practices and sustainable operations are more likely to thrive over the long run. By considering nonfinancial factors, they aim to identify investments better positioned to weather social and environmental challenges.

Influence and Advocacy

Biblically based and ESG investors may use their shareholder influence to advocate for positive change within companies. They can engage in dialogue with corporate management, submit shareholder resolutions, and participate in proxy voting to encourage companies to adapt better practices that align with their values.

Biblically based investing and ESG may be complementary investing approaches with similar values and objectives. By investing in biblically sound companies that operate according to ethical and socially responsible practices, investors can align their investments with their Christian beliefs and values while positively impacting the environment, society, and governance.

14

Heaven, Earth, and the Prosperity Doctrine

Although they sound similar, biblical prosperity and the prosperity gospel are two different concepts related to prosperity and wealth. Depending on the interpretation, some embrace the elements of the prosperity gospel. In contrast, others reject it as inconsistent with the broader teachings of the Bible.

Prosperity Doctrine

The prosperity doctrine has gained significant attention in recent years, attracting both fervent supporters and ardent critics. Also known as the prosperity gospel or the health and wealth gospel, this religious belief teaches that financial wealth and physical health are signs of God's favor and blessings. It suggests that if a person has faith and gives generously to the church, God will bless them with wealth and good health. Believers can claim wealth and abundance through faith and positive confession.

This doctrine teaches that Christians are entitled to financial and other blessings from God and that those who experience financial hardship or illness simply lack sufficient faith or are not giving enough to their church. This belief system suggests that financial abundance is a sign of spiritual and moral favor from God.

Critics of the prosperity doctrine argue that it places too much emphasis on material wealth and ignores the importance of spiritual growth, character development, and self-sacrifice. They also suggest that the prosperity doctrine can lead people to feel guilty or ashamed if they experience financial struggle or illness, as if these circumstances result from their lack of faith.

In contrast, many Christian groups emphasize the importance of generosity, responsible financial management, and serving others without expecting financial rewards or blessings in return. They believe that while God may bless some with financial abundance or good health, these are not the ultimate indicators of God's favor or blessing.

Contrasting the Prosperity Doctrine

While the true riches of heaven focus on spiritual blessings and eternal rewards, the prosperity doctrine emphasizes material wealth and temporal success as a sign of God's favor. It is essential to discern the difference between biblical prosperity, which includes spiritual growth and contentment, and pursuing riches solely for personal gain.

The Bible teaches that true wealth is not measured by earthly possessions but by your relationship with God and your treasure stored in heaven. The prosperity doctrine can sometimes lead to the love of money, which is warned against in scripture as it can lead people away from the true faith. Your contentment should come from knowing God and trusting in His provision rather than being solely focused on material gain.

Jesus teaches the importance of humility and detachment from earthly riches, encouraging you to seek the kingdom of God first. Keeping an eternal perspective reminds you that your ultimate goal is not wealth and prosperity on earth but the inheritance and blessings of God's kingdom.

> So we fix our eyes not on what is seen, but on what is unseen, since what is seen is temporary, but what is unseen is eternal (2 Corinthians 4:18, NIV).

Biblical Basis of Prosperity

Biblical prosperity encourages believers to find contentment in God's provision, to be generous and compassionate, and to trust in God's sovereignty and eternal perspective. It teaches that true prosperity encompasses spiritual growth, emotional well-being, and healthy relationships, recognizing that God's blessings go beyond material possessions and financial success.

Secret of Abundance

Jesus offers abundant life to believers. This fullness of life primarily pertains to spiritual abundance and eternal life rather than material wealth.

> The thief comes only to steal and kill and destroy. I came that they may have life and have it abundantly (John 10:10, ESV).

God can and does bless people materially, but it also emphasizes spiritual prosperity, character development, and seeking God's will above all else. Ultimately, biblical prosperity aims to glorify God and pursue His will rather than placing undue emphasis on worldly wealth and personal gain.

It doesn't mean God doesn't want you to have material blessings on earth, but it's about the heart and what you treasure most. Paul describes it well.

> Not that I am implying that I was in any personal want, for I have learned how to be content (satisfied to the point where I am not disturbed or disquieted) in whatever state I am. I know how to be abased and live humbly in straitened circumstances, and I know also how to enjoy plenty and live in abundance. I have learned in any and all circumstances the secret of facing every situation, whether well-fed or going hungry, having a sufficiency and enough to spare or going without and being in want (Philippians 4:10–12, AMPC).

Faith vs. Positive Confessions

Like motivational speakers, prosperity gospel preachers use the art of power of positive thinking and confession. They encourage believers to speak positive words and affirmations to attract blessings and success. While positive thinking has its benefits, it is essential to remember that the Bible teaches the importance of humility, contentment, and acknowledging the sovereignty of God. Faith pleases God.

> And I tell you, ask, and it will be given to you; seek, and you will find; knock, and it will be opened to you (Luke 11:9, ESV).

> And whatever you ask in prayer, you will receive, if you have faith (Matthew 21:22, ESV).

Christian Journey

Becoming a Christian isn't a ticket to no more suffering here on earth. The prosperity doctrine doesn't account for suffering and hardships in a believer's life. It often implies it is because the person lacks faith or isn't generous enough. Your wealth or lack thereof doesn't determine whether you will suffer or not. Jesus warned that believers will experience hardships.

> I have told you all this so that you may have peace in me. Here on earth you will have many trials and sorrows. But take heart, because I have overcome the world (John 16:33, NLT).

True Riches of Heaven Contrast the Prosperity Doctrine

The true riches of heaven are far more valuable and lasting than material possessions or worldly achievements. Your hope is not solely fixed on the temporary pleasures of this life but on the eternal glory that awaits you in the presence of God.

Eternal Life

One of the most profound promises in the Bible is eternal life through faith in Jesus Christ. This is not merely a prolonged existence but an everlasting life filled with joy, peace, and the fullness of God's presence.

> For God so loved the world that he gave his one and only Son, that whoever believes in him shall not perish but have eternal life (John 3:16, NIV).

Joy and Peace

In heaven, believers will experience the fullness of joy and peace, free from the troubles and sorrows of this world—no more tears.

> And God will wipe away every tear from their eyes; there shall be no more death, nor sorrow, nor crying. There shall be no more pain, for the former things have passed away (Revelation 21:4, NKJV).

Presence of God

Heaven's ultimate reward is being in God's eternal presence, worshipping and glorifying Him forever. Your relationship with God will be complete, and you will experience the depths of His love and glory.

> No longer will there be a curse upon anything. For the throne of God and of the Lamb will be there, and his servants will worship him. And they will see his face, and his name will be written on their foreheads (Revelation 22:3-4, NLT).

Rewards for Faithful Service

You will be rewarded in heaven for faithful service and obedience to God during your time on earth. These rewards are not based on material wealth but on the impact of your actions and the motives behind your service. God looks at the heart.

> For the Son of Man is going to come in the glory (majesty, splendor) of His Father with His angels, and then He will render account and reward every man in accordance with what he has done (Matthew 16:27, AMPC).

> Don't store up for yourselves treasures on earth, where moth and rust destroy and where thieves break in and steal. But store up for yourselves treasures in heaven, where neither moth nor rust destroys, and where thieves don't break in and steal (Matthew 6:19–20, CSB).

A New Body

In the resurrection, believers will receive glorified bodies, free from sin, sickness, and death. These new bodies will be imperishable and suited for the eternal nature of heaven.

> But our citizenship is in heaven. And we eagerly await a Savior from there, the Lord Jesus Christ, who, by the power that enables him to bring everything under his control, will transform our lowly bodies so that they will be like his glorious body (Philippians 3:20–21, NIV).

Fellowship with Believers

In heaven, believers will experience the joy of being reunited with loved ones who have also trusted in Christ. Moreover, they will enjoy perfect fellowship with all other believers from various nations and generations.

> Then we who are alive and remain shall be caught up together with them in the clouds to meet the Lord in the air. And thus we shall always be with the Lord (1 Thessalonians 4:17, NKJV).

After this I looked, and there before me was a great
multitude that no one could count, from every nation,
tribe, people and language, standing before the throne and
before the Lamb. They were wearing white robes and were
holding palm branches in their hands. And they cried out
in a loud voice: "Salvation belongs to our God, who sits on
the throne, and to the Lamb" (Revelation 7:9–10, NIV).

Ultimately, the true riches of heaven are centered on the person of Jesus
Christ, who is the Way, the Truth, and the Life. Only through Him can you
receive eternal life and all the blessings God has prepared for you in heaven.

15

Generosity and Tithing

Generosity and tithing are timeless practices that resonate deeply with the human spirit, transcending religious dogma and cultural barriers. In a world that often seems fragmented and divided, the principles of generosity and tithing serve as unifying forces, bringing people together under the banner of love and concern for one another.

As you embrace the spirit of giving, you embark on a journey of spiritual growth, discovering the transformative power of selflessness and compassion. Generosity and tithing bless the recipients and enrich the givers' lives, fostering a profound sense of fulfillment and purpose.

Generosity Principles Shared by Different Religions

Generosity is a universal virtue that is shared among different religions. They all emphasize the importance of generosity as an act of worship, compassion, gratitude, and selflessness. These shared principles reveal that generosity is not just about giving money but also about positively impacting others' lives and reflecting the ultimate example of love and selflessness.

By embracing generosity as a core value, kingdom builders live more meaningful and purposeful lives rooted in faith and service.

Giving to Those in Need

Giving without expectations of receiving something in return is fundamental to generosity. As a kingdom builder, you are called to help those in need through financial contributions, volunteer work, or other means. Jesus taught that caring for the poor and marginalized is a central aspect of Christian discipleship.

> The generous will themselves be blessed, for they share their food with the poor (Proverbs 22:9, NIV).

Tithing and Sacrificial Giving

You are encouraged to give a portion of your income to support the work of the church and other nonprofit organizations. General tithing refers to 10 percent. The Bible also teaches the value of sacrificial giving, where individuals give beyond what is comfortable or convenient. Sometimes generosity requires the sacrifice of giving up what you value the most or need.

> Whatever you give is acceptable if you give it eagerly. And give according to what you have, not what you don't have (2 Corinthians 8:12, NLT).

Hospitality and Service

Compassion motivates generosity. It is caring and showing kindness toward others. Generosity requires selflessness, the willingness to put others' needs and interests ahead of yours. Practicing hospitality and serving others may involve offering food, shelter, and emotional support to those in need and participating in community service projects and outreach programs.

> Share with the saints in their needs; pursue hospitality (Romans 12:13, CSB).

RYAN BOURQUE, CPA, MBT, CKA

Generosity as a Spiritual Discipline

Being grateful for what you have encourages generous sharing. Generosity is a form of spiritual discipline. By intentionally giving your time, talents, and resources, you can cultivate a spirit of generosity and grow in your faith.

> Honor the Lord with your capital and sufficiency [from righteous labors] and with the firstfruits of all your income (Proverbs 3:9, AMPC).

Defining Generosity and Tithing

Generosity and tithing are two essential concepts regarding Christian stewardship and giving. Generosity emphasizes the spirit behind giving, while tithing refers to a specific percentage of income given to maintain the church.

Generosity refers to the state or quality of being generous, freely giving or sharing, and showing a willingness to give freely without expecting to receive anything in return. Generosity comes from the heart and is more than just giving money. It goes beyond material possessions and encompasses giving others your talents, time, and resources. Generosity reflects gratitude for what God has done for you and your willingness to share what you have with others.

Tithing is a concept that is found throughout the Old and New Testaments. The word *tithe* means one-tenth and refers to a percentage of your income or possessions given to the church. Tithing is an act of obedience to God. It is intended to support the church's ministry and enable it to fulfill its mission.

According to the book of Leviticus, tithing means giving one-tenth of your annual income or resources to the Levites for the temple's upkeep. Jesus Himself affirmed the practice of tithing, as recorded in the Gospels.

"Well, then," Jesus said, "give to Caesar what belongs to Caesar, and give to God what belongs to God" (Mark 12:17, NLT).

This form of generosity is an ancient practice embraced by many religions and cultures throughout human history. Tithing is seen as an act of faith and generosity that benefits the individual and the community.

Tithing is not limited to a specific religious denomination. It is also practiced by Muslims, who call it *zakat*, and by many other faiths and traditions worldwide. The amount that you should tithe varies among religions and cultures.

One of the main benefits of tithing is that it provides a sense of purpose and fulfillment. Giving to others makes you feel that you are contributing to a greater good and positively impacting the world. Tithing also serves as a reminder that wealth is not only for personal consumption but also for the betterment of society.

Tithing also has financial benefits, encouraging you to manage your finances wisely. When you set aside a portion of your income for donations or charitable causes, you become more mindful of your spending habits and tend to avoid frivolous expenses. Moreover, tithing can also help you establish financial security as you develop a habit of saving and investing that can benefit you in the long run.

In addition to spiritual and financial benefits, tithing also promotes a sense of community and social responsibility. When kingdom builders come together to give generously, you create mutual support and care networks. Tithing can inspire others to give, creating a ripple effect that benefits numerous causes and organizations.

However, tithing can also become problematic if done out of obligation or guilt. For example, some religious organizations may pressure their members to tithe, which can create feelings of resentment and misgiving. Tithing should be done willingly, without the fear of punishment or the expectation of reward.

Tithing is timeless with numerous benefits, spiritually, financially, and socially. Develop a habit of setting aside a portion of your income or resources to support charitable causes and give back to your communities. Tithing can help you find fulfillment and joy while supporting those in need and improving the world.

Importance of Generosity and Tithing

Generosity is a central concept in Christian life. It is a way of serving and loving your neighbors. Generosity reflects the nature of God, who gave His only Son for you. Giving from a generous heart is not only a blessing to the recipients but also a blessing to the giver. Generosity helps you to grow in your faith and to develop a trusting relationship with God.

Tithing is an act of obedience to God's command and expressing gratitude for His blessings. Tithing enables the church to fulfill its mission, support its ministry, and share the gospel with others. Tithing is not only about giving money but also about giving your trust and faith to God. When you tithe, you acknowledge that everything belongs to God and that He is the source of your blessings and resources.

After Abraham's victory in battle, he meets Melchizedek, a priest of God who blesses him. In response, Abraham gives Melchizedek a tenth of everything he has. Hebrews 7:1–10 argues that Levi, the priestly line of the Israelites, tithes to Melchizedek through Abraham. It demonstrates the superiority of Christ's priesthood, which is not based on the law of Moses but on the power of an indestructible life.

> Then Melchizedek king of Salem brought out bread and wine; he was the priest of God Most High. And he blessed him and said: "Blessed be Abram of God Most High, Possessor of heaven and earth; and blessed be God Most High, Who has delivered your enemies into your hand. And he gave him a tithe of all" (Genesis 14:18–20, NKJV).

God commands the Israelites to tithe their crops, herds, and flocks. The tithe is to be holy and consecrated to God.

A tithe of everything from the land, whether grain from the soil or fruit from the trees, belongs to the Lord; it is holy to the Lord. Whoever would redeem any of their tithe must add a fifth of the value to it. Every tithe of the herd and flock—every tenth animal that passes under the shepherd's rod—will be holy to the Lord (Leviticus 27:30–32, NIV).

Jesus rebukes the Pharisees for tithing their spices but neglecting justice, mercy, and faithfulness. He tells them to practice tithing but not neglect the law's more important matters. Jesus tells the Pharisees that they tithe their mint, rue, and herbs but neglect justice and the love of God.

Woe to you, scribes and Pharisees, hypocrites! You pay a tenth of mint, dill, and cumin, and yet you have neglected the more important matters of the law—justice, mercy, and faithfulness. These things should have been done without neglecting the others (Matthew 23:23, CSB).

Robbing God

God rebukes the people of Israel for not tithing and promises blessings to those who do.

Malachi, a prophet, lived in the fifth century BC, during the Persian period of Jewish history. The Jewish people had returned from exile in Babylon and were rebuilding Jerusalem and the Temple. However, many people were struggling in the new circumstances, facing social and economic hardship. The priests and leaders were also seen as corrupt and unfaithful to God.

"Should people cheat God? Yet you have cheated me!" But you ask, "What do you mean? When did we ever cheat you?"

> "You have cheated me of the tithes and offerings due to me. You are under a curse, for your whole nation has been cheating me. Bring all the tithes into the storehouse so there will be enough food in my Temple. If you do," says the Lord of Heaven's Armies, "I will open the windows of heaven for you. I will pour out a blessing so great you won't have enough room to take it in! Try it! Put me to the test!

> "Your crops will be abundant, for I will guard them from insects and disease. Your grapes will not fall from the vine before they are ripe," says the Lord of Heaven's Armies. "Then all nations will call you blessed, for your land will be such a delight," says the Lord of Heaven's Armies (Malachi 3:8–12, NLT).

In this context, Malachi speaks to the people and calls them to greater faithfulness and obedience to God. He specifically addresses the issue of tithing, which refers to giving a tenth of one's income or produce to the temple or religious community. The passage argues that withholding tithes and offerings is equivalent to robbing God and contributes to the nation's spiritual and material problems.

However, Malachi also promises blessings to those who repent and return to obedience, including the abundance of food and protection from pests and crop failure. The passage ends with a vision of Israel being blessed and becoming a model nation for the world.

Tithing is as relevant today as in ancient times. God doesn't need the money; it's an act of worship, acknowledging that everything belongs to God and giving back a portion of what He gave you.

Financial Blessings

Many people believe that tithing can lead to financial blessings. Some people have shared stories about how they started tithing and suddenly gained more financial stability or received unexpected bonuses or job promotions. You don't tithe to be blessed but to honor God. Tithing is a biblical principle; therefore, you are blessed because you are obeying God's command.

Improved Relationships

Tithing isn't just about giving money to a church or organization; it's also about giving back to the community. Some people believe that tithing has helped them strengthen their relationships with others in their community by providing opportunities to serve and connect with others.

Spiritual Fulfillment

Tithing is an act of faith that provides spiritual fulfillment. People have shared stories about how tithing has helped them feel more connected to their faith and their purpose in life.

Personal Growth and Development

Tithing can also be a way to invest in personal growth and development. By giving back to others, people can develop communication, leadership, and empathy skills that can benefit all areas of life.

While the blessings of tithing may vary from person to person, giving back to God can positively impact your life and those around you.

Generosity and tithing are two essential concepts in Christian stewardship. Generosity reflects your gratitude to God and willingness to share what you have with others. Tithing is an act of obedience to God's command to support the church's ministry. Both concepts are not only about giving money but also about sharing your talents, time, and resources with others. As Christians, it is important to learn to be generous with your blessings and tithe to faithfully support the church's ministry.

16

Stewardship of Influence and Affluence

Influence and affluence are two powerful tools God entrusted to His followers. As a kingdom builder, you are called to shift your perspective from ownership to stewardship, recognizing that God is the ultimate owner of all things and that your position of influence and wealth are not ends but gifts entrusted to you by God. Stewardship of these tools requires faithful and responsible management that honors God and serves others.

The Stewardship of Influence

Stewardship of influence is recognizing your sphere of influence, understanding your impact in your personal and professional lives, and using it for God's kingdom. Living as an ambassador of Christ, you embrace your responsibility of representing Christ in your interactions and sharing the love and truth of the gospel. With personal growth and character development, you ensure your influence aligns with God's values.

The purpose of Influence is to speak up for those who don't have influence.

—Rick Warren

Influence is connecting with others in meaningful ways that help them to grow. It is not for your benefit but to benefit others. The purpose of influence is to speak up for those who don't have any influence. King Solomon's prayer in Psalm 72 was for more influence to support the widow and orphan and protect and care for the oppressed and those with no voice.

It is about character and integrity more than popularity, power, and prestige. Influence is not a position, authority, or fame. You can be a famous celebrity with little influence. It's not affluence either; having money doesn't necessarily give you influence. Your character, an essential kingdom builder leadership criterion, makes your influence valuable, not your position or title. Serving others and generosity is the way to more significant influence.

> Not so with you. Instead, whoever wants to become great among you must be your servant (Matthew 20:26, NIV).

You cannot be a kingdom builder without being a person of influence desiring to make a difference. Your circle of influence—family, friends, relatives, neighbors, and business—is a gift from God that you should use to impact others positively. It's an opportunity to be a generous giver. What you do with your influence determines if it grows. In Exodus 4:2, God asked Moses what was in his hand. You have something you are good at God can use to expand your influence.

If you aren't influencing others, they are affecting you.

> This is how the Lord responds: "If you return to me, I will restore you so you can continue to serve me. If you speak good words rather than worthless ones, you will be my spokesman. You must influence them; do not let them influence you" (Jeremiah 15:19, NLT).

Jesus didn't allow others to influence Him; He did His Father's will. A kingdom builder does the right thing, even when others disagree.

"Teacher," they said, "we know that you speak and teach what is right and are not influenced by what others think. You teach the way of God truthfully" (Luke 20:21, NLT). To gain influence, people must trust you, and then they will listen to what you have to say. Be truthful and live a life of integrity. Love your neighbor and pray for people. Being a steward of influence also means people will like you and others will criticize you.

The Stewardship of Affluence

Christian leaders have long advocated a generous heart regarding the stewardship of affluence. Gospel artist Mandisa Hundley, known as Mandisa, said:

When I give of my resources, I am really able to be a great steward over what God has given me.

Every time you open your wallet, you are casting a vote for the kind of world you want.
—Rick Warren, *The Purpose Driven Life*

Warren reminds his readers that generosity is crucial to serving others and should be done cheerfully and willingly.

You must each decide in your heart how much to give. And don't give reluctantly or in response to pressure. For God loves a person who gives cheerfully (2 Corinthians 9:7, NLT).

Fostering an attitude of gratitude for the resources and blessings you received and contentment for what you have and don't have helps avoid the pitfalls of greed, materialism, and a poverty spirit. Nurturing financial stewardship by adopting wise financial practices, including budgeting, saving, and giving generously, leads to responsible wealth management.

The key to stewardship of affluence is understanding the power of intentional and sacrificial giving, supporting causes that align with God's heart, and advancing His kingdom through your financial resources, which belong to God anyway.

Stewardship Insight from Rick Warren's Life

Pastor Rick Warren is someone who walked the walk and talked the talk. Through his successes, he has grown in abundance of wealth and influence. He gave the invocation for President Obama's inauguration. He hosted a presidential forum at Saddleback Church with John McCain and Barack Obama. He was *Time* magazine's listed America's pastor because of his impact and influence in America.

Pastor Rick decided to reverse tithes and increased his tithing in giving over the years to reach 90 percent ultimately—he gave away 90 percent and lived on 10 percent. He drove a green Ford Expedition for the better part of twenty years, so much so that the paint was going and the wheels and transmission were about to fall out of the car. In an article between himself and Warren Buffet, he was dubbed as one of the people who lived simply and humbly despite financial success.

He used his influence to further the cause of Christ and to grow the kingdom on earth more so than anybody I've read about or come in contact with. His life is a model to follow, and I can't think of anybody who did a better job in this modern age of trying to live like Christ by the example we were given. Based on his teachings and writings on stewardship and living a purposeful Christian life, these five insights influenced me as a kingdom builder.

Gratitude and Contentment

Approach affluence with a grateful and content heart. Rather than being consumed by pursuing material wealth, recognize and appreciate the blessings of prosperity while remaining content with what God has provided.

Responsible Management

Responsible management of financial resources is crucial. You must develop wise financial habits, including budgeting, saving, and giving generously. By managing affluence responsibly, you can honor God and utilize your resources to positively impact the world.

Purposeful Giving

Giving is a significant expression of stewardship. Use your financial resources to support causes that align with God's heart and advance His kingdom. Generous and intentional giving is an essential aspect of stewarding affluence in a way that reflects God's love and compassion for others.

Influence for God's Purposes

Recognize and steward your influence for God's purposes. Use your position of influence to positively impact others, share the gospel, and transform your community. Stewarding influence involves living as an ambassador of Christ, representing Him well in all areas of life.

Alignment with God's Will

Align affluence and influence with God's will and purposes. Seek God's guidance and direction in utilizing your resources and influence, ensuring that your decisions and actions follow biblical principles and values.

SECTION 3

TAXES

17

Blessings in Tax Breaks

At times, it may look like the IRS is targeting successful kingdom builders who achieve financial prosperity. However, the truth is simpler—the agency's primary goal is to collect as much as possible for the government. Regardless of the political climate, your profile rises on their radar the more money you make.

A May 2022 report from the United States Government Accountability Office revealed that taxpayers with an earned income of $5 million or more were the primary focus of audits in 2020 (for tax year 2019).

You might benefit from adopting debt-reducing federal policies instead. Regardless, for the foreseeable future, taxes are an inevitable part of every kingdom builder's growth journey.

However, you can legally reduce the amount you are assessed to owe the IRS by strategically utilizing the tax code, following Christ's principles of generosity. For example, you can make capital gains taxes an optional cost—an option implemented by Congress.

My firm specializes in tax controversy (or helping clients survive audits as painlessly as possible), but clearly, this is not ideal. I prefer seeing people keep their tax lives in order, reducing auditors' interest—and limiting how much they are assessed to owe.

Tax mitigation and the more aggressive tax avoidance strategies involve legally planning out your personal income and business taxes to utilize earned credits and deductions, thereby limiting your tax liability.

Minimizing vs. Evading Taxes

Tax mitigation involves ethical and forward-thinking stewardship principles. For optimal results, tax mitigation requires long-term planning. Short-term, single-year approaches won't generate the same savings as comprehensive, long-term strategies. By optimizing your personal and business taxes, you can minimize your tax liability and keep your financial affairs in order, reducing the likelihood of audits.

For example, by thoroughly examining your kingdom builder business and personal finances, you may identify potential reductions ranging from $500 to $5,000 on your current year's tax bill. While this may sound appealing, it is merely a fraction of what could be achieved by adopting a strategic approach to manage your tax liability over the next ten years.

Embracing this perspective when dealing with your business and personal taxes maximizes your savings potential. Moreover, there are additional benefits beyond financial gains, like giving generously.

Charity's Hidden Blessings

As a Christ-minded kingdom builder, you likely embrace philanthropy and your commitment to giving to godly charities goes beyond tithing. Understanding that worldly possessions cannot compare to the treasures stored in heaven, your philanthropic efforts can have both spiritual and practical impacts. In the realm of practical benefits, engaging in philanthropy can lead to various tax credits and deductions. The Internal Revenue Service (IRS) recognizes tax-exempt organizations, specifically 501(c)(3) charities, providing corporate donors with the opportunity to deduct up to 25 percent of their taxable business income as a form of governmental reward. For individual donors, the tax benefits can be even more significant. While there are limitations on standard deductions—60 percent of AGI itemized on Form 1040—qualified personal donations to 501(c)(3) charities can be deducted for up to 100 percent of your adjusted gross income (AGI). This generous deduction allows you to maximize the financial impact of your charitable contributions. The IRS stipulates specific criteria to ensure that your contributions qualify for these deductions. The donations must be in cash (not assets), given to recognized 501(c)(3) organizations, and made within the last calendar year.

A charitable gift annuity is an excellent example of philanthropy with long-term financial benefits. This arrangement involves making a generous donation to a charity. In return, you (or you and your spouse) receive a fixed income for life. The charity invests your donation, generating the income that supports your regular payments.

You receive monthly or quarterly payments based on your age at the time of donation. Moreover, the remaining gift amount goes to your chosen charity upon your passing. When you donate, your tax deduction is determined by estimating the total amount the organization will eventually receive after fulfilling all annuity payments.

Furthermore, some of the income you receive from the annuity may also qualify for tax-free status for a certain period. This time frame is calculated based on statistics, indicating your likely life expectancy.

By combining your faith-driven desire to serve others and support godly causes with sound financial stewardship, you can profoundly impact both the spiritual and material realms through strategic philanthropy and wise tax planning.

Gifts That Keep Growing

Donating appreciated assets, including long-term securities like stocks, bonds, and mutual funds, can be a powerful way to support your favorite causes while maximizing tax benefits. Unlike cash donations, these gifts have the potential to keep growing in value, benefiting both the charitable organization and your tax deductions. When you donate stock, you can

RYAN BOURQUE, CPA, MBT, CKA

typically claim a deduction for its full fair market value. This means you get a tax break based on the assessed value of the stock at the time of donation. Additionally, by donating appreciated stock you've held for over a year, you can avoid paying capital gains taxes on the appreciation. This way, your chosen charity receives a more substantial gift (as much as 20 percent more) than if you sell the asset first and donate the cash after paying capital gains taxes. The same tax advantage applies to mutual funds and bond donations, making them attractive options for charitable giving.

Another strategy that can provide tax benefits is a like-kind exchange, a 1031 exchange. While commonly used by business real estate owners to defer capital gains taxes on property sales, this method can also be utilized for charitable giving.

You can avoid immediate capital gains taxes by selling a property and reinvesting the proceeds into another property of similar value. However, it's important to note that noncommercial properties, such as your primary residence or vacation home, do not qualify for this type of exchange. The replacement property doesn't have to be identical to the sold property. Still, it should be within the same category, such as both being business or investment properties. It's essential to have owned the old property for at least a year before the exchange occurs.

There are two specific time constraints to be aware of. You have forty-five days from the old property's sale date to identify potential replacement properties. This must be documented, with written notification to the seller and a qualified intermediary (who cannot be your attorney, banker, realtor, accountant, relative, or employee). The purchase of the new property must be completed within 180 days of selling the old property or before the due date for your tax return (whichever comes first).

By utilizing these strategies and donating appreciated assets, you can significantly impact your favorite causes while optimizing your tax situation responsibly and legally.

Inter Vivos Advantages

In the realm of charitable giving, there's a smart strategy available to you once you've owned a property for over a year. You can make an inter vivos gift of a new property to a charity—an expression in legal terms for a donation made while alive. This approach can be particularly beneficial when avoiding substantial capital gains taxes that might arise from a nonexchange sale. By doing so, you serve God's kingdom through your generosity and reap financial benefits.

One effective way to carry out this kind of charitable giving is by donating a property acquired through a 1031 exchange to a donor-advised fund (DAF). This charitable vehicle accepts irrevocable gifts from donors and then distributes those funds to selected organizations on their behalf. As a donor, you can contribute up to 90 percent of the property's value to your DAF. This generous act results in a federal tax deduction equivalent to the current fair market value of the real estate, up to 30 percent of your adjusted gross income (AGI). However, if the property's value exceeds 30 percent of your income, you don't lose out; any excess can be carried over to future tax returns for up to five years.

As a dedicated kingdom builder, you have a plethora of tax advantages available to you through charitable giving. By understanding the major tax benefits for both personal and business philanthropy, you can make a meaningful impact on the causes you care about while enjoying potential financial benefits.

18

Foundations, DAFs, and You

Establishing a private foundation is one of the most straightforward and effective ways to approach your charitable giving, prioritizing both the kingdom and potential tax benefits. This type of nonprofit organization can be funded by you, your family, or your kingdom business and is governed by a board of trustees or directors responsible for making and managing grants to your chosen causes.

The advantages of a private foundation extend beyond just time-saving benefits. For instance, the funds you contribute to the foundation have the potential to grow over time, enjoying tax-deferred status due to the foundation's 501(c)(3) designation. While it may be more accurate to refer to it as "tax-deferred" rather than "tax-free," this status can significantly enhance the growth and impact of your charitable gift.

By strategically utilizing a private foundation, you can efficiently channel your philanthropic efforts, making a meaningful difference in causes you support while maximizing potential tax benefits. The long-term growth of the foundation's assets can provide lasting support for charitable endeavors, embodying the essence of giving to God's kingdom.

Complication-Free Control

Moreover, a significant advantage of utilizing a trust for charitable giving is that you and your family maintain complete control over the organization without any intermediary involvement. This level of control translates to increased flexibility in managing the trust's assets. Additionally, since a trust is recognized as a separate legal entity, it offers a degree of liability protection, providing you with an added layer of security.

Depending on your residence, there may be exclusive tax benefits for trusts. Some states may allow you to bypass capital gains or income taxes related to your trust, providing potential tax savings. However, it's essential to remember that no earthly investment vehicle is without its considerations. For private foundations, there is an annual excise tax on net investment income exceeding $500. Though this tax is typically around 2 percent, its financial impact is generally negligible compared to the overall benefits.

While some initial expenses may be involved in launching and capitalizing a trust, its subsequent steady income often justifies these costs. Adhering to regulatory and oversight requirements is essential, but much of this involves basic accountability measures to ensure proper governance.

By harnessing the power of trust for your philanthropic endeavors, you can maintain control, enjoy greater asset management flexibility, and potentially access exclusive tax benefits while creating a lasting impact for the causes you cherish. Though certain considerations must be considered, the advantages of utilizing a trust can far outweigh any associated challenges.

Donor-Advised Funds (DAFs)

Donor-advised funds (DAFs) have a fundamentally different structure that sets them apart from private foundations. Like foundations, DAFs also accept irrevocable gifts, but they present a more straightforward and cost-effective option for starting your charitable giving journey.

Unlike private foundations, where you retain control over the funds, a DAF assumes ultimate control of the assets you donate. Some DAFs provide flexibility by allowing you to advise on allocating funds to specific charities according to your preferences. Others may have a preapproved list of charities, limiting your choices to the organizations they support.

Here's an example to illustrate how a donor-advised fund works.

Let's say Andre decides to donate $15,000 to a charity. Andre establishes a donor-advised fund with an organization that sponsors DAFs, typically a financial institution or community foundation, and contributes $15,000.

The sponsor opens Andre's DAF account and records its creation for tax purposes. Immediately, Andre receives a deduction from the IRS for the entire $15,000 gift in that tax year, as the charitable contribution is recognized.

Over time, the $15,000 gift is invested strategically to achieve long-term growth. Andre can then recommend allocations from the DAF to various 501(c)(3) charities. If approved, he can choose to distribute the funds instantly or allow them to grow until a later date.

At a certain point, Andre grants $3,000 to a specific cause. He submits a recommendation to the DAF sponsor, specifying the recipient and the amount. The sponsor reviews his recommendation and verifies the selected cause's tax-exempt status with the IRS. Assuming the DAF sponsor approves, $3,000 is donated on Andre's behalf, reducing the balance in his DAF account accordingly.

Andre can contribute additional funds for future grants to the donor-advised Fund, potentially netting additional tax benefits.

By utilizing a donor-advised fund, you can efficiently manage your charitable giving, receive immediate tax benefits for your donations, and retain influence over where your contributions are distributed. This streamlined approach offers a practical and effective way to support the causes you care about most.

Strategizing Appreciated Assets

Appreciated stocks and bonds can also be donated to a DAF. This means that Andre can select a security to gift to present alongside instead of money. Just as it did in his portfolio, it can continue generating returns, growing his DAF account. This could potentially last for years.

For instance, suppose Andre bought 1,500 shares of WidgetCo, a publicly traded company, a few years ago at $7 per share. If he decides to sell those shares outright and donate the cash, the IRS will assess his capital gains as $50,000. If the current federal capital gains tax rate is 15 percent, he will owe $7,500.

Giving the IRS their due means his DAF will receive $42,500 ($50,000 x 15 percent). That is nearly *$8,000* less than they might receive if he donates his WidgetCo stock instead of selling it. Since there is no federal capital gains tax on charitable donations, Andre can expect a tax deduction for the full value of $50,000.

Furthermore, by donating an appreciated asset, the DAF receives a dynamic contribution that has the potential to grow over time, generating additional returns. The growth within the DAF account accumulates tax-free, making it a highly advantageous choice for gifting to a 501(c)(3) charity. Suppose Andrew plans to sell a mature holding from his personal portfolio soon, he could opt to donate multiple other assets, generating multiple deductions. Strategically planning his donations this way allows Andrew to offset his capital gains tax from the sales, providing a comprehensive tax-saving approach.

By leveraging the benefits of donating appreciated assets to a DAF, Andre can maximize the impact of his philanthropy while enjoying substantial tax advantages. This thoughtful and strategic approach to charitable giving aligns his financial goals with his desire to support meaningful causes.

Taxing Situations

The IRS sets a limit on appreciated securities donations, capping it at 30 percent of your adjusted gross income (AGI) for the 2022–2023 tax year. If Andre has held the assets for at least a year, he can deduct their fair market value up to this 30 percent threshold. Once a qualified appraiser confirms the exact amount, he can utilize this deduction immediately.

Alternatively, Andre may reserve the deduction for a year with a higher tax liability if it falls within five years from the donation date. However, some states, like California, may not offer this flexibility for their state taxes. Capital gains taxes on securities in California's top brackets can be as high as 50 percent, making it an unfavorable option to sell the position and donate the proceeds. This could result in Andre paying half of his annual income in state capital gains tax, which would not benefit him, the donor-advised fund, or his chosen charity.

Furthermore, California treats all residents' short-term and long-term capital gains as regular income, disregarding the distinctions made by the U.S. Internal Revenue Service. Consequently, all capital gains are taxed at the state's regular income tax brackets.

These are compelling reasons why donating securities to a donor-advised fund is generally a more advantageous option than selling them and gifting the proceeds. The chosen charity receives the largest possible gift, undiminished. The donated assets can continue to grow tax-free, providing additional benefits over cash donations. Donors can avoid heavy federal and state tax costs associated with selling the assets. Sizable deductions become available for immediate use or can be strategically utilized later.

By donating appreciated securities to a DAF, Andre can maximize the impact of his giving, take advantage of tax benefits, and provide invaluable support to the causes he cares about without incurring excessive tax liabilities.

Downside of DAFs

Donor-advised funds (DAFs) are often seen as a more egalitarian option for charitable giving since multiple parties can donate even in smaller amounts. However, this approach comes with trade-offs, particularly when it comes to freely choosing causes that align with your values.

Conducting due diligence and thoroughly researching the DAF and its provider before committing is crucial. While the IRS grants some tax advantages to DAFs similar to private foundations, DAFs do not have the same obligation to make annual distributions. Unlike foundations, a DAF is not compelled to donate to your chosen charities each year once you have selected them. This can potentially result in a situation where a philanthropist pays their financial professional for little more than looking busy.

Moreover, some DAF providers impose their own policies on donations. Some may require donors to give every year even though no tax regulations mandate such a practice. This can add another layer of complexity and limitation to your giving strategy.

One aspect where DAFs are often praised is their ability to provide a higher level of privacy. Participants can remain anonymous, giving donors a sense of discretion. However, this anonymity can sometimes lead philanthropists to unknowingly align financially with donors whose fundamental values conflict with their own.

To navigate these challenges, donors must carefully assess their priorities, research potential DAF providers thoroughly, and seek clarity on the policies and requirements of the chosen fund. Donors can make more informed decisions by ensuring that their charitable giving aligns with their values and maximizes its impact.

Faithful Financial Decisions

Undoubtedly, charitable giving offers significant tax benefits regardless of the chosen approach. For a devoted kingdom builder, the key lies in discerning the most effective way to utilize the funds they steward. As with any decision of great importance, embarking on the path of charitable giving begins with prayer.

By seeking God through prayer, you can gain clarity and direction in your philanthropic endeavors. He guides and empowers you to make wise decisions, selecting the most impactful and meaningful charitable giving options that align with your kingdom builder values and mission.

Giving becomes more than just a financial transaction; it becomes an intentional and purposeful journey of making a positive difference in the lives of others and advancing the kingdom's values. Trusting in the guidance received through prayer, as a kingdom builder, you can confidently embark on your charitable journey, knowing that your actions are aligned with God's purpose and deeply rooted in faith.

19

Charitable Remainder Trust (CRT)

Charitable remainder trusts (CRTs) are unique trusts offering an income stream for you or a beneficiary of your choosing for a designated period. At the same time, the remaining portion of your donation is reserved to benefit your chosen charity after your passing.

The two main CRT types are charitable remainder annuity trusts (CRATs) and charitable remainder unitrusts (CRUTs). With CRATs, you donate a lump sum or contribute assets to the trust. In return, you receive a fixed annuity annually. It's essential to plan ahead since additional contributions cannot be made to a CRAT after the initial donation.

Unlike CRATs, CRUTs offer more flexibility as you can make multiple donations. The income you receive from the trust is evaluated annually, adjusting to reflect a percentage of the trust's current value.

By donating appreciated assets from your portfolio to either type of trust, you can benefit from tax-deferred growth. Furthermore, the value of your gift is determined based on its current market value at the time of donation, potentially offsetting capital gains taxes. For instance, if you were to sell an asset from your portfolio with a significant profit, donating it to a CRT could help mitigate the impact of capital gains taxes.

In addition to the tax benefits, a CRT can offer asset protection, shielding your assets from lawsuits, creditors, or financially irresponsible family members. For business owners and entrepreneurs, a CRT can play a valuable role in the sale of their business, lowering the capital gains rate on profits and providing a steady stream of income for the beneficiary. Since a CRT is tax-deferred, you are exempt from paying taxes on the sale. CRTs offer a strategic and rewarding approach to charitable giving, benefiting the donor and the chosen charity while serving as a powerful financial planning tool.

One crucial caveat to be mindful of is the timing of including a CRT in your business sale planning. It's essential to consider this trust during the early stages of the process. Suppose you already have a potential buyer in mind and attempt to incorporate the CRT later. In that case, the IRS may view it as forcing the trustee to sell to that individual.

Unfortunately, if the prearranged sale doctrine comes into play, all the anticipated tax benefits associated with the CRT will be immediately revoked. This can lead to unexpected financial consequences, leaving you at a disadvantage.

Planning your business sale with the CRT in mind from the outset is crucial to avoid this potential pitfall. By carefully considering the trust's inclusion early in the planning stages, you can ensure that you retain valuable tax benefits and safeguard yourself from any unforeseen financial setbacks.

By being proactive and strategic in your approach, you can effectively maximize the advantages of the CRT while safeguarding your financial interests during the business sale process.

A charitable remainder trust (CRT) serves as a philanthropy-focused cornerstone of an estate plan, offering a compelling simplicity in donating real estate or stocks in exchange for a lifetime of steady income. The appeal of lower estate taxes upon passing and reduced income taxes presently makes this approach even more attractive.

However, it's essential to recognize that a CRT may not suit everyone's circumstances. With some organizations' economic challenges, identifying the causes to support can become more challenging for philanthropists.

There is a viable solution if you are drawn to a CRT but are torn between supporting multiple charities. By naming foundations or donor-advised funds as CRT beneficiaries, you can alleviate the pressure and have the freedom to explore other pursuits.

This approach can also contribute to a family legacy beyond monetary contributions. If a DAF receives a mature security that continually replenishes the account, family members and descendants can continue the tradition of giving for generations to come, speaking volumes to the future.

Your financial advisor can assist in managing the DAF's investments after your passing, creating a lasting platform for ongoing donations. In the meantime, by donating money from your CRT, you can avail yourself of tax deductions and allocate funds for immediate grants as you see fit.

Occasionally, you may desire to expedite your CRT to give more generously sooner. In such cases, donors can close out your CRT entirely into a DAF or cash out your income interest for a significant tax benefit.

Kingdom business is both a long-term and present endeavor. Through charitable giving, as you prioritize God's will, you can benefit from financial advantages by utilizing legitimate tax-reducing opportunities. These opportunities, like accumulated cents and dollars, lead to daily rewards and reinforce the principles of kingdom-minded stewardship.

20

Kingdom Business and Charitable Deductions

The preceding chapters may have sparked thoughts of potential tax benefits from the future sale of your business, even if that date lies years ahead. However, the advantages of charitable giving extend far beyond this, benefiting kingdom businesses everywhere, every single day.

In 2 Corinthians 9:7, the apostle Paul reminds us that the Lord loves a cheerful giver, highlighting the inherent joy and fulfillment of giving generously. But beyond the immediate satisfaction of being a cheerful giver, taking a long-term approach to strategically generate tax deductions and credits throughout your business operations can lead to additional tangible benefits.

When kingdom business is executed in surrender to Christ, it enables a beautiful integration of your life's spiritual and professional aspects. By granting the Lord control in every sector, you align yourself with His will and create a fertile ground to receive His blessings for your obedience.

This harmonious marriage of faith and business elevates the impact of your efforts, infusing them with a more profound sense of purpose and meaning. It empowers you to serve not only your own interests but also the greater good of others, ultimately contributing to the advancement of God's kingdom.

As you embrace the concept of strategic and intentional giving, you unlock a profound synergy between your faith-driven principles and the practicalities of business. In doing so, you discover a wellspring of blessings that extend far beyond financial rewards, enriching your life and those you touch in immeasurable ways.

Fidelity's Fulfillment

I often emphasize to my clients the importance of taking a 360-degree approach to tax planning. This holistic view considers all aspects of their financial life in true 3D. This enables my team and me to strategically leverage upcoming tax credits from their business side to reduce capital gains on the sale of retirement portfolio assets in the future, creating a seamless and efficient tax planning strategy.

A practical tax planning approach involves the freedom to navigate between business and personal finances. Similarly, as a kingdom builder business leader, the more territory you surrender to God, seeking His will, overlapping areas lead to more incredible blessings for His kingdom, yourself, your businesses, and those in need.

While the IRS is not God's physical embassy on earth, it is reasonable to consider that lowered taxes due to charitable giving may be a part of His blessings for you. Corporate philanthropy can yield as many tax benefits as personal charitable giving, making it a valuable avenue to explore financial opportunities.

However, it is essential to avoid giving solely for public approval, as Jesus sternly warns against such actions in Matthew 6:2. Instead, pray for discernment, seek guidance from the scripture, and patiently wait for His direction. Donating to an organization merely because it is popular can lead to poor stewardship in the long run.

By aligning your financial decisions with your values, seeking God's guidance, and taking a comprehensive approach to tax planning, you can navigate the complexities of your business and personal finances while reaping blessings beyond financial benefits. Kingdom-minded stewardship opens doors to fulfilling God's purposes and positively impacting others and the world around you.

Due Diligence

As Paul wisely points out in 1 Corinthians 14, God is not a god of confusion. Charitable urges are often from His Holy Spirit, but not all the charities in the world today are worthy vessels. Therefore, after praying for discernment, conduct thorough research on a prospective cause before donating.

Better Business Bureau's Give.org page (https://give.org/) is a valuable resource to find helpful information and ratings on various charities. Additionally, you can visit the IRS website and use the Tax Exempt Organization Search Tool, which provides access to filed Form 990s of all 501(c)(3) charities. These forms offer insights into each charity's mission, finances, and operations, including details about their board of directors and independence.

When reviewing Form 990, check sections 3 and 4, as they indicate the voting members of the governing body and the number of independent members respectively. Moreover, don't forget to explore Schedule O, which may provide essential explanations and insights into the charity's day-to-day operations. Annual reports and audits of candidate charities can also be valuable sources of information. However, depending on their size and resources, they may not always be available for every organization.

By conducting this diligent research and seeking transparent information, you ensure that your charitable giving aligns with your values and makes a meaningful impact globally. Making informed choices in your giving allows you to be a good kingdom builder steward of the resources God entrusted to you. It ensures that your contributions positively contribute to advancing His kingdom.

Kingdom Builder Strategic Philanthropy

Embarking on this elaborate process of strategic giving may seem daunting at first, but the results can be gratifying. Donating to a charity sends a powerful message for your kingdom business. It can have a remarkable impact on your branding and public image. While authenticity should always be the driving force behind your giving, the positive exposure it generates can set your company apart and create a lasting impression in the hearts of your audience.

In a world where actions speak louder than words, strategic philanthropy becomes a valuable marketing asset that even the most skilled marketing firms can only dream of replicating. When you carefully and faithfully select organizations that align with your values and receive the Lord's blessings, the good imparted to everyone involved can be truly remarkable.

Following God's plan in your giving can lead you to support causes that impact the community around you and resonate with the demographic you serve. Aligning your business with charitable efforts that reflect your brand's essence can create a win-win-win scenario—serving the kingdom, establishing your brand identity, and reaping tax benefits.

Moreover, adopting a kingdom-focused, long-term tax planning approach can alleviate the financial burden of purchasing expensive necessities for your business, such as equipment, machinery, or software. Instead of watching these assets depreciate rapidly, there are smart solutions that can help you make the most of your investments.

Consider the example of Jane Kingdombuilder, a well-established small business owner. While focusing on short-term tax reduction might seem tempting, this shortsighted approach overlooks potential deductions that could save her from $500 to $5,000 on her current year's tax bill.

By integrating strategic giving and long-term tax planning, you can maximize the impact of your business decisions, align them with your faith, and create a lasting legacy of generosity that extends far beyond mere financial gains. Ultimately, this intentional approach allows you to effectively steward your resources, fulfilling your purpose of advancing the kingdom and leaving a positive imprint on the world.

Winning the Long Game

However, the potential for tax liability strategizing over the next ten years goes far beyond the examples mentioned earlier. Jane Kingdombuilder can leverage her business milestones to generate deductions that can be utilized on her personal returns. For instance, she might plan to expand her staff in two years, earning valuable credits or deductions for hiring qualified candidates from IRS-recognized at-risk groups.

Additionally, Jane could consider expanding the parking lot of a commercial real estate holding in her retirement portfolio to enhance its appeal to future renters. If her construction company is involved, she can even hire her own business for the expansion, creating yet another tax deduction while boosting the potential revenue of her real estate retirement asset.

Another important aspect of tax planning is the flexibility to carry forward deductions to future tax years. Jane could choose to retain the real-estate-improvement tax break and apply it in a year when her profits have increased, pushing her taxable income into a higher tax bracket. This strategic timing can yield more significant savings.

Furthermore, Jane could explore other opportunities to lower her overall tax bill. For example, while itemizing her business lunches used to allow a 100 percent deduction in 2022, it has been reduced to 50 percent for the tax year 2023. Nonetheless, every deduction counts, and the cumulative effect of multiple deductions can still be substantial.

Investments in expensive equipment, software, or machinery for her construction company can also be advantageous. She may claim up to 70 percent of the equipment's bonus depreciation in 2024, enabling her to use a large single deduction for a significant tax break rather than spreading smaller deductions over time.

Considering the long-term impact of these deductions and investments on Jane's business finances and tax situation is essential. While opting for a larger single deduction isn't always the best strategy, periodic investments in essential assets depreciating over time can still provide valuable tax benefits.

Incorporating thoughtful tax planning into her business decisions can empower Jane to optimize her financial situation, maximize her tax savings, and ultimately be a responsible steward of her resources. By strategically aligning her business and tax goals with her faith values, Jane can build a legacy of wise financial stewardship and kingdom impact.

Consider a Business Foundation Too

Starting a foundation through your kingdom builder business can offer numerous benefits and create a more comprehensive approach to your philanthropic efforts. In addition to the positive impact of private giving, a corporate foundation opens up new avenues for generating tax benefits and strategically managing your contributions.

One of the key advantages of a foundation is the flexibility it provides in varying your annual contributions. You can give more generously during prosperous times, creating a reserve to navigate leaner periods when essential expenses and operations may require additional funding.

Moreover, a foundation allows for a more structured approach to philanthropy. You can tailor its operating policies to efficiently manage grants, screen requests, and support causes that align with your company's culture and strengths. This streamlines the favoring of charitable initiatives that resonate with your organization's mission.

Beyond the public message of giving back, a charitable foundation can significantly impact employee morale. Demonstrating a commitment to the community and supporting causes close to your employees' hearts fosters a sense of purpose and teamwork within the company. Implementing periodic charitable-donation-matching programs further reinforces the company's dedication to making a difference.

A corporate foundation also allows responding swiftly in times of crisis or need. By issuing emergency grants to support employees during disasters or establishing a scholarship program to aid in their personal development, you can illustrate compassion and genuine care for your workforce.

Starting a foundation through your kingdom builder business can create a more robust and meaningful approach to charitable giving. It amplifies the positive impact of your philanthropy. It showcases your company's values and commitment to making a difference in the world.

Ownership Inspires Philanthropy

Employee stock ownership plans (ESOPs) offer a range of advantages worth considering. ESOPs encompass various defined contribution plans, including profit sharing, stock bonuses, money purchase (retirement) plans, and 401(k)s. In this context, we specifically focus on granting employees company stock outright.

Through ESOPs, employees receive benefits equivalent to their account balances, including contributions made by the company. Suppose your ESOP is part of a larger plan, such as profit sharing, and employees can contribute. In that case, they can divest their stock to other plan investments after a specified period.

Beyond fostering loyalty and enhancing productivity, ESOPs can provide tax deductions, effectively reducing your overall tax burden. Some deductible examples include cash contributions for stock purchases within the ESOP, the value of company stock offered through the ESOP, and cash used for principal payments on loans taken to fund stock purchases.

Additionally, a stock ownership program can offer unexpected benefits, such as assisting with estate planning by lowering estate tax liability. If you, as the owner of a closely held corporation, sell enough stock to your ESOP so that it owns 30 percent or more of the company, you can defer the tax implications.

KINGDOM BUILDERS PLAYBOOK

By implementing an ESOP, you not only incentivize your employees and gain tax advantages but also pave the way for effective estate planning. ESOPs can be a strategic tool to ensure the long-term success and financial well-being of your business and your employees.

Timing a 1042 Exchange

A powerful tax-saving strategy in employee stock ownership plans (ESOPs) is the 1042 ESOP rollover or 1042 exchange. This mechanism allows you to roll the proceeds from selling company stock into similar U.S. operating company stocks or bonds, effectively deferring and, in some cases, eliminating applicable capital gains taxes. Your sell stock must meet the IRS criteria for qualified securities to qualify.

The tax benefits of the 1042 ESOP rollover can extend beyond your lifetime. If the replacement stock is held until your passing, the favorable tax treatment transfers to your heirs on a stepped-up cost basis. This special provision recognized by the IRS and many states' revenue departments ensures continued tax advantages for your loved ones.

Engaging in an ESOP arrangement can also address succession issues by avoiding potential conflicts with third parties. By selling your interest in the company to an ESOP, you create a seamless transition that upholds the established culture and philosophy of the business. This fosters continuity and stability, promoting long-term success.

Moreover, an ESOP serves as a powerful employee incentive program. Employees who become partial owners through the ESOP have a personal stake in the company's achievements. This shared sense of ownership motivates them to work collectively toward the organization's prosperity, creating an energized and dedicated workforce.

The benefits don't stop there. An ESOP can also inspire employees to give back to their communities. As they participate in charitable giving, their chosen causes benefit society, generate employee cash flow, and result in tax deductions. Furthermore, the recipient charity receives an additional cash bonus when the ESOP buys back the stock.

Incorporating an ESOP into your kingdom builder business can unlock many financial advantages, promote a positive workplace culture, and foster a sense of purposeful giving among your employees. By embracing this approach, you are not only benefiting your business but also impacting the broader community in a meaningful way.

Conclusion

I would also like to extend my gratitude to the publishers, editors, and designers who have worked tirelessly to bring this book to life. Your dedication and expertise have been invaluable in shaping the content and presentation of this book.

To all the readers, thank you for choosing to embark on this journey of becoming kingdom builders. I sincerely hope that the insights and guidance provided in this book have been helpful to you in your pursuit of leadership, investing, stewardship, and navigating the complexities of taxes.

Throughout the chapters, you have explored various topics and principles essential for building a solid foundation in each area. Each page has sought to equip you with the tools necessary to thrive in all aspects of life, from understanding the importance of integrity, the art of strategic thinking, to the power of generosity and giving.

As you conclude this book, I want to impress upon you the significance of applying these principles not only for personal success but also for the advancement of God's kingdom here on earth. By embracing true leadership, wise investing, responsible stewardship, and wise tax strategies, you can make a lasting impact and leave a legacy beyond your life.

Remember, building a kingdom is not a solitary endeavor. It requires collaboration, teamwork, and a shared vision. Let us strive to build a community of kingdom builders committed to using our resources and influence for the greater good.

In closing, I encourage you to continue seeking knowledge, wisdom, and understanding. Surround yourself with mentors and like-minded individuals who will challenge and inspire you. And above all, never lose sight of the ultimate purpose and calling we have as kingdom builders—to honor and serve God in all we do.

May this book serve as a valuable resource and guide as you navigate the complexities of leadership, investing, stewardship, and taxes. May you be filled with the courage and conviction to step into your role as a kingdom builder and make a difference in the world.

Thank you once again for joining me on this journey. May you find joy, fulfillment, and success as you embrace the principles outlined in this book. Together, let us build a kingdom that reflects love, integrity, and a commitment to making the world a better place.

God bless you abundantly in all your endeavors.

Ryan Bourque, CPA, MB.T, CKA

References and
Recommended Resources

1. Alcorn, Randy. 2017. *The Treasure Principle: Unlocking the Secret of Joyful Giving* Revised Edition. Multnomah.
2. Blue, Ron. 2016. *God Owns It All: Finding Contentment and Confidence in Your Finances.* Lifeway Press.
3. Blue, Ron. 2016. *Master Your Money: A Step-by-Step Plan for Experiencing Financial Contentment.* Moody Publishers.
4. Blue, Ron. 2017. *Never Enough?: 3 Keys to Financial Contentment.* B & H Books.
5. Green, David. 2017. *Giving It All Away … and Getting It All Back Again.* Zondervan.
6. Green, David. 2010. *More Than a Hobby: How a $600 Startup Became America's Home and Craft Superstore.* Thomas Nelson.
7. Prelec, D., Simester, D. *Always Leave Home Without It: A Further Investigation of the Credit-Card Effect on Willingness to Pay.* Marketing Letters 12, 5–12 (2001). https://doi.org/10.1023/A:1008196717017
8. Ramsey, Dave. 2011. *EntreLeadership:20 Years of Practical Business Wisdom from the Trenches.* Howard Books.
9. Reeb, Lloyd. 2004. *From Success to Significance: When the Pursuit of Success Isn't Enough.* Zondervan.
10. Rees, Erik. 2006. *S.H.A.P.E: Finding and Fulfilling Your Unique Purpose for Life.* Zondervan.
11. Warren, Rick. 2010. *The Purpose Driven Church.* Revised Edition. Zondervan.
12. Warren, Rick. 2002, 2011, 2012. *The Purpose Driven Life.* Zondervan.

Printed in the United States
by Baker & Taylor Publisher Services